"FREEHAN'S BOOK IS FAR MORE CANDID AND REVEALING THAN BOUTON'S"*

"Freehan's book is far more candid and revealing about the "insides" of baseball than Bouton's. So if baseball fans want to get inside the scenes of baseball's current controversy, I suggest they pick up Freehan's book and go BEHIND THE MASK"
        —John Bentley, KFRA, San Francisco*

"Well worth reading . . . inside information you don't find anywhere else"
        —*Terre Haute Tribune*

BEHIND THE MASK

Bill Freehan

An Inside Baseball Diary

Edited by
Steve Gelman and Dick Schaap

POPULAR LIBRARY • NEW YORK

Dedication:

FOR ALL THE PEOPLE WHO HELPED
MAKE A DREAM A REALITY

Introduction

DON'T
DROP
THIS ONE,
DUMMY

The ball spun off Tim McCarver's bat and sailed high in the air, halfway between home plate and first base. I flipped off my mask, moved out from behind the plate and set myself to catch the pop-up, just as I'd caught a thousand pop-ups before.

But this one was different.

It was the bottom of the ninth inning of the seventh and final game of the 1968 World Series, and my team, the Detroit Tigers, was leading the St. Louis Cardinals, 3-1. There were two men out and no men on base, and all I had to do was catch this pop-up and, for the first time in twenty-three years, only the third time in history, the Detroit Tigers would be the world champions of baseball.

All I could think was: "You've had a bad World Series. Now don't drop this one, dummy."

I'd come into the World Series off a strong 1968 season —twenty-five home runs, more than I'd ever hit before, and eighty-four runs batted in, more than I'd ever driven in before. I'd won the Gold Glove as the best fielding catcher in the American League for the fourth year in a row. I'd been the American League's All-Star starting catcher for the third year in a row. I'd played well enough to finish second in the voting for the American League's Most Valuable Player for the second year in a row.

But in the Series, I'd committed two errors in seven games—over my career, I'd averaged only one error each twenty-five games—and I'd managed only two hits in twenty-four times at bat, a batting average of .083, about 180 points below my lifetime average.

Yet as I circled under that pop-up, I didn't care whether I'd had two hits or twenty in the World Series. I just wanted to squeeze that ball and find out what it felt like to be a world champion.

I caught the ball.

The World Series was over.

The Detroit Tigers were champions of the world.

For six seasons, I'd been a major-league catcher, playing baseball for the fun of the game, for the satisfaction of doing something well and for the money I earned, and, suddenly, with one simple little catch, I discovered what I'd really been playing for all the time: the great, glorious glow of knowing you're Number One.

Three months have passed now since the 1968 World Series—three short, rewarding months. I collected roughly $11,000 as my winning share in the World Series. I've earned more than $30,000 from endorsements and speeches and all the fringe benefits that come from being a winner.

And now, at the age of twenty-seven, I'm ready for another spring training, the first that I've ever gone to as a member of a world championship team.

I'm proud of what we've accomplished, and I'm worried, too. I wonder whether we're hungry enough, whether all we've gained since the World Series has made us complacent. I wonder whether all the outside interests we've acquired by being champions are going to detract from our main interest, are going to keep us from concentrating, as we should, on baseball.

I don't know the answers. I do know that I want to win again, that now that I've tasted the champagne of World Series victory, nothing less will ever satisfy me again.

Keeping this diary is my idea—no one else's. I really love baseball, and there's a lot I'd like to say about the game, a lot I've never read anywhere, a lot that most people just don't know. People often ask me, "What's it like behind the mask?" Well, I think my viewpoint, the catcher's viewpoint, is unique. I'm the only man on the field who's directly involved with the hitters, with the pitchers, and with the manager. I'd like to get that special viewpoint across in my diary. I don't know what the closing scene'll be, but I'll never forget the closing scene of 1968:

I awoke the morning after we won the seventh game of the World Series, and my head was buzzing from the champagne, and I looked out my window, and there on my lawn was a long line of children and nuns from the local Catholic school. They were all singing. They were singing, "We Love You, Freehan."

—BILL FREEHAN
Detroit
January, 1969

1

LOOK
AT THE
MONSTER
MAN

February 26

At 10 A.M. today, when a bunch of the Detroit Tigers ran out on the field at our spring training camp in Lakeland, Florida, I became a holdout. I watched the guys run out. I wasn't in uniform. I hadn't signed any contract. The general manager, Jim Campbell, and I hadn't been able to come to an agreement on my 1969 salary.

We hadn't even done much negotiating because of a dispute between the major-league owners and the Major League Baseball Players Association—our union, I guess you'd call it—over the funding of our pension plan. Campbell told me a few days ago that he wouldn't negotiate with me, as a matter of principle, unless I promised to sign my contract by March 1. I told him that I wouldn't sign my contract, as a matter of principle, until the owners and the Association reached an agreement. But I wanted to negotiate anyway, so that as soon as the dispute was settled, I could sign my contract and climb into uniform. "Maybe we can get a jump on some of the other teams that way," I told Jim. "Anything to help us win again."

Jim and I did toss a few figures around. He asked me how much I wanted, and I told him $60,000, up from the $37,000 I got last year. I knew it was a big raise, but I felt it was fair, based on what I'd heard and read that other catchers—like Tim McCarver of the Cardinals and Joe Torre of the Atlanta Braves—were getting.

Jim said that he was thinking of a salary a little closer to $50,000. He gave me his best offer, his top figure, and said he couldn't compromise. I told him I couldn't compromise either, because my wife, Pat, was getting used to living the good life. I told Jim I couldn't come home with less than Pat was planning to spend.

We didn't get really serious until yesterday, when the owners and the Association settled. Then we had a long talk early this morning on the telephone, but neither of us indicated any willingness to compromise. "I'm going out to the ball park, anyway," I told my wife after breakfast. "Just to watch. Got to see which young kids want to come and steal my job."

At 10:30 A.M. I started looking for Jim Campbell. I knew I was going to give in first. I think he knew it, too. He knows how much I like to play this game. "Let's compromise," I said, when I found him. "I'll sign for your figure if you'll agree to give me a $2,000 bonus if I make the All-Star team and a $3,000 bonus if we win the division title." Each of the major leagues is divided into two divisions this year, an Eastern and a Western, and the division winners will play off for the league championship.

Jim said he couldn't write bonus clauses into a contract, that it was against league rules. We talked some more, and each of us compromised a little.

At 11:15 A.M., I signed my contract, walked into the clubhouse, put on my number 11 uniform and stood there with a big old smile on my face. My holdout had lasted exactly seventy-five minutes.

February 27

Norm Cash and I were sitting together in the clubhouse today. Norman's been our regular first baseman for the past nine years, and in 1961, his second year with us, he batted .361 and led the American League in hitting. He's never hit .300 since then. "The only mistake I made in my whole baseball career," he likes to say, "was hitting .361 that one year, because ever since then people have expected me to keep on doing it." At least I think that's what Norman likes to say. He comes out of Texas and when he talks, he sounds like he's gargling the Rio Grande.

Norman's always got something to say, no matter how he says it. Once, during a batting slump, he struck out, and when the fans booed him, he took off his hat and saluted them. Then he came back to the dugout, threw off his hat and helmet, and said, "Boys, things got so bad out there that time even my wife was up there booing."

Norm and I got to talking about our off-season work, how we'd spent the winter. It really was lucrative this year, as a result of winning the World Series. I signed a contract to do advertising and public-relations work for the Dodge people and another to do customer-relations work for Vernor's Bottling, a soft-drink company. I made commercials for Moto-Ski snowmobiles and the National Bank of Detroit, and, generally speaking, I moved myself up into the interesting financial brackets. Just about everybody on our team did pretty well, of course, but the big winners were two of our pitchers, Denny McLain and Mickey Lolich. Denny, who won thirty-one games last year—nobody had won thirty games in the major leagues since Dizzy Dean back in the 1930s—must've earned close to $100,000 during the off-season, and Mickey, who beat the Cardinals three times in the World Series, couldn't have been too far behind.

Norman, who was our leading hitter in the World Series, told me he'd spent most of the winter working as a public-relations man for a Fort Worth bank. "Learned something, too," he said. "Figured out how to keep from losing money with bad stock or business investments. Only way you keep from losing money with bad investments is to spend it."

I think that's what Norman said.

March 1

We heard today that Mickey Mantle announced at the Yankee training camp he's quitting baseball, and we all felt a little sad. I don't know how many times he's beaten us, how many times he's taken money out of our pockets, but we're going to miss him.

In a way, we ought to be glad he's quitting, because the Yankees are in our division, along with Baltimore, Boston, Cleveland, and Washington, and without Mantle, even a sore-legged Mantle, the Yankees are a weaker team. But you hate to see a guy like that retire. Mickey brought very special talent, courage, and excitement to a ball game.

I remember when they had a Mickey Mantle Day at Yankee Stadium four or five years ago. He collected a pile of gifts and made a brief, modest speech. Later, when Mickey came to bat, our pitcher, Joe Sparma, walked off the mound and up to home plate. "You know, I've never had a chance to meet you in person," Joe said to Mickey, "and I've always admired you." Mickey stuck out his hand, and Joe shook it, and then Joe walked back to the mound and struck Mickey out.

Mantle turned around to me and said, "They have a day for me and your manager's got to put some hard-throwing kid out there." Mickey grinned. "Couldn't he have put in some soft-tossing left-hander for me to hit off of," Mickey said, "so I could look like a hero in front of all those people?"

The Yankees are going to miss Mantle. Now if only Frank Robinson, Brooks Robinson, and Boog Powell would retire from the Baltimore Orioles, we'd be in pretty good shape in our Eastern Division.

March 3

Except for Willie Horton, our home-run-hitting outfielder, all of our regulars are signed and in camp, so today our manager, Mayo Smith, held his first team meeting. I enjoy playing for Mayo. He gives me a lot of personal authority in a game and rarely second-guesses the way I run things and call signals.

Mayo's low-key, quiet, thoughtful, not easy to anger. He's not a strict disciplinarian—he treats us like men—and he's not an orator. He didn't try to give us any big inspirational speech. He simply said that he wanted us suited up at the ball park by ten o'clock every morning and in bed by midnight every night. He said that last year we worked hard in the spring and paid attention to fundamentals and, during the season, those fundamentals—hitting behind the runner, throwing to the right base, holding men on, sacrificing—were the keys to our championship. He said he wants us to work hard on fundamentals again. "Let's go get 'em," he said, and the meeting was over.

Afterward, one of the Detroit newspapermen came over to me and we talked about the "Tiger Finish," our trademark in 1968. We came from behind more than forty times to win games last year; we were down in the World Series, three games to one, and 3-0 in the fifth game, before we bounced back. "After watching you guys last year," the newspaperman said to me today, "I'll never give up on the Detroit Tigers again."

I've stuck that one in the back of my mind.

March 4

I've learned to pace myself in spring training, to ease myself into shape. The first few days, I just loosened up all the muscles, just tried to limber up without straining myself, but now we're into more strenuous training. We started off with calisthenics at ten—I usually lead the team in jumping jacks, push-ups, sit-ups, running in place, nothing too tough for a washed-up old football player like me—followed by about twenty minutes of playing pepper. Then we split up into groups—infielders, outfielders, pitchers, and catchers—for individual drills.

I put on all my equipment—shin guards, mask, chest protector, metal cup—and Hal Naragon, who coaches our catchers, threw about fifty balls into the dirt, one right after the other, so that I could practice blocking low throws. When a ball's in the dirt and a runner's on third base, you don't have time to think; you just have to stop the ball and that run.

After the individual drills, I caught batting practice, working here, too, at learning to do things by instinct again—not to blink when a batter swings and misses, not to flinch on a foul tip. Then I hit for a while, knocked off at a quarter to one, and started running.

We're supposed to do ten wind sprints from the right-field foul line to the center-field wall. After the required wind sprints, I did a little extra running, from foul line to foul line about half a dozen times. Then, on my own, I did some sit-ups and some special exercises to strengthen my back. When I first came up to the Tigers, some of the older players accused me of doing this extra work to show them up. "Gung ho," they called me. "The rah-rah-rah kid from college."

I used to go out of my way to convince them that I simply believed the unusual demands of catching—the constant popping up and down, the constant throwing, those sprints down the line to back up first base—forced me to work extra hard to get into condition. Now I don't try to convince anyone of anything. I'm only concerned with one thing: getting Bill Freehan in shape to play the 1969 baseball season.

March 5

Gates Brown, our super sub—he batted .462 as a pinch hitter last year—is having trouble getting into shape. Gate's five-foot-eleven and usually plays at about 215 pounds, but he's way over that now. The guys have been calling him "Buffalo," but Gates doesn't seem to mind the kidding. "I've got a little belly and the pitchers'll try to jam me," he says, "but I'll be on time with the bat."

Gates never seems self-conscious about anything. The Tigers spotted him when he was playing baseball in a penal institution around Mansfield, Ohio; I think we signed him on his way out, which explains his nickname. One day, after he'd been with us a while, he and Willie Horton got to discussing the relative merits of the high schools they'd attended. "I got a much better education," Willie said. "I took all kinds of good courses. What did you take in high school, Gates?"

"I took a little English," Gates said, "a little mathematics, some science, some hubcaps, some wheel covers."

March 7

We played our first exhibition game today, against Pittsburgh in Bradenton, and the Pirates beat us, 6-2, breaking our three-game World Series winning streak. Only 29 more preseason games, 162 regular-season games, and 2 summer exhibition games to go. If we do well enough in those games, we get to play a three-out-of-five series for the American League championship and then a four-out-of-seven series for the world championship. Just think: if we're lucky, we get to play 205 baseball games in the next 220 days.

There's nothing in the world I'd rather do than play baseball, but that's ridiculous.

March 9

With banners and pregame ceremonies and the lengthiest invocation I've ever heard from a Catholic priest, Lakeland saluted the world champion Detroit Tigers today. This was our first home exhibition, and the priest blessed everything and everybody, especially me. The guys know I'm Catholic, and they kept winking at me during the invocation. "Now I know how you've been doing it all these years," said Cash. "With all those prayers, you can't help but be successful."

I hit a three-run home run and we whipped the Minnesota Twins. I wonder if there's a parish open in Detroit for that priest?

March 12

I was talking with a few newspapermen this morning about Willie Horton, who was the last Tiger to sign and come to camp. I'd heard Willie was asking for $100,000—about triple his 1968 salary—but I imagine he settled for considerably less. One of these seasons, I told the reporters, Willie's going to hit a hundred home runs, and I won't be all that surprised. I meant it. Willie's got the talent to be a real superstar. He's got to be one of the strongest men in the world.

We first met when we were about thirteen years old, and Willie was almost as big then as he is now. (He's not too tall—only about five-foot-ten, but the most solid five-foot-ten you ever saw.) We played against each other on the Detroit sandlots. In one game, he tried to run me over at the plate, and I tagged him out, and we began rolling over and grabbing at each other. A bunch of people poured on the field and pulled us apart, and I wasn't too unhappy about being pulled away from Willie. Someone told me he was an undefeated Golden Gloves fighter then, and I believe it. He's tough. I'm afraid he's going to get mad some day at some pitcher who's knocked him down and, before we can get enough guys to restrain him, he's going to go out and just pinch that pitcher's head off. ⟶

Willie's moody sometimes, hard to figure out sometimes, but basically, I like him. He's a good fellow. He rooms with Gates Brown, and once last year, when we were staying at a motel somewhere, Mayo Smith called their room at midnight to see if they had both gotten in by curfew. The call woke Willie up.

"Willie?" the manager said. "Gates there? I want to talk to him."

Willie was still half-asleep. "Just a minute," he said. "I'll see where he is."

Gates wasn't in the room, and Willie, waking up, realized that his roomie was liable to get hit with a $1,000 fine for missing curfew. Willie started thinking. He took three minutes thinking, and then he came back to the phone.

"Well, he's not here," Willie said.

"What took you so long to look around the room?" Mayo said.

"Well," said Willie, "I couldn't find him in the bedroom, so I looked in the bathroom, and he wasn't there. And then I looked in the closet, and he wasn't there. And then, Skip"—Willie started talking fast—"I found a note. Gates left a note and it says he just stepped out to the ice machine, and he'll be right back. Don't worry, Skip, he'll be right back."

March 15

Denny McLain has been taking flying lessons. He's imported an instructor from Detroit to give him lessons here, and we've been calling him "Sky King" or sometimes, because he won the Cy Young Award last year, "Sky Young."

Denny sort of flies in his own world anyway—I guess just about everybody knows that he spends as much time playing his Hammond organ as he does playing baseball —so none of us mind him flying around down here. If he's got to learn to fly, I'm glad he's using the skies over Lakeland instead of the skies over Detroit. It's less crowded here, and I'd sure hate to lose a thirty-one-game winner.

But some of us were pretty resentful today because, while the rest of us traveled down to Miami by bus—our only overnight trip of the spring—Denny flew his own plane down. Mayo's got a strict rule that the whole team has to travel together, and it's almost impossible for any of us to get permission to violate that rule. Denny's excuse—that he wanted to practice his flying—just didn't seem good enough to some of us.

We were kind of unhappy, too, because we played the Baltimore Orioles tonight, and they beat us pretty badly. Everybody hit the ball for them, and nobody hit it for us. This is the only time we face them all spring, and I'd hate to have them leave Florida believing they're going to run away from the world. They're our chief competition in the Eastern Division of the American League. We beat them by twelve games last year, but they were missing Frank Robinson part of the season, and Brooks Robinson and Boog Powell didn't have particularly good years. They're going to be tough. They're a good team. I just hope we're a little better.

March 18

We've played eleven exhibition games so far, and we've lost six of them. I'm not worried about our record—we lost more than half our exhibitions last year, and we went on to win more regular-season games than any Detroit team in history—but I am worried about the way we're playing.

The object of exhibition games is to look over your new fellows, let the regulars work themselves into condition, and get everybody into good playing habits. We've been getting into bad habits. It's not just that we've had weak hitting and sloppy pitching. It's that we've been making little errors, mental errors, the kind that can make the difference between victory and defeat in tight games. We've been cutting off throws when we should've let them go through; we've been letting them go through when they should have been cut off. These are fundamentals, the kind of things Mayo stresses, and we should be doing them properly now, right from the beginning. Last year, we were magicians, geniuses. Every decision we made—bunt, hit away, cut off a throw, let it go—everything seemed to work out our way. I wish they'd start working now. We've got to wake up. We've got to be alert. We've got to get into smart habits.

March 19

We've had a lot of rain lately and some of our pregame workouts have been canceled, so this morning I decided to go up to the park early for some extra batting practice. Jim Northrup, one of our outfielders, a good solid hitter, went with me. My wife and my two daughters and I are living in a cottage apartment on the outskirts of Lakeland, and Jim and his family live nearby. We often share the ten-minute ride to the park.

Jim's one of my closest friends on the club. He's a battler; he hates to lose. He's also one of our best ballplayers. Jim's got a few nicknames. We call him "The Gray Fox," for his silver hair, and "Sweet Lips," for his golden words. He's the king of the caustic comment. "Lay some sweet words on me, Sweet Lips," we like to say.

Jim and I got to the park around 8:30 and, after I pitched to him for fifteen minutes, he went out to the mound to pitch to me. I set myself in the batter's box, and Jimmy started to wind up. Then I decided to readjust my stance and I looked down at my feet. Jimmy had already thrown the ball.

I still had my head down when the ball reached the plate. It caught me right on the bridge of my nose, next to my left eye. The ball hit hard, and the nose cracked, and blood began pouring down my face.

I ran for the locker room, trailing blood. I knew I'd broken my nose, no doubt about it. The question was how severely. Getting my nose broken was nothing new to me, but this time I suspected that I'd really done a good job.

Bill Behm, our trainer, and Don McMahon, a relief pitcher, drove me to the Watson Clinic, three blocks away. A doctor X-rayed the nose and confirmed that it was broken. He had to set it. He stuck some splints inside the nose, put an aluminum splint on the outside, cleaned it, and packed it with cotton. He had to reset it in about ten places and you could hear and feel things just crack. I came out with my whole face covered with tape, except for two eyeholes. The doctor gave me some Darvon pills and said the pain would be pretty bad.

The trainer drove me back to the park and a couple of guys asked what happened. I told them. "Unbelievable," one of them said. "That's what you get for trying to work a little extra hard."

I telephoned my wife. "Hey, honey," I said. "You know that vacation we've been talking about?"

"Yes."

"Well, we can take it. We can go anywhere we want for at least ten days."

"What do you mean?" she said.

"I broke my nose."

"You what?"

"I broke my nose and the doctor said I won't be ready to play until opening day. That's about three weeks from today."

My wife used to be a nurse, but when I got home, with my face all taped up, she was shaken. My kids—Corey, four, and Kelley, three—ran outside. All afternoon as I was trying to rest, they kept bringing their playmates in to "look at the Monster Man."

March 20

I'm taped up like a mummy. I can't eat. I have to settle for liquids. I can't see too well, either. My left eye is all black and blue, and my vision is blurred. The team played the Boston Red Sox today in Winter Haven, and as I listened to the game on the radio, I spent a lot of time thinking about their rightfielder, Tony Conigliaro. Tony got hit by a pitch two years ago and temporarily lost his vision in one eye. He seems to be okay now, but he missed all of last season.

I've had a lot of injuries—broken noses, broken fingers, dislocations, hairline fractures. In high school, the last game of my senior year, I had to have ten stitches in my right hand after a runner spiked me while I was tagging him out at the plate. In college, I needed thirteen stitches when a guy tore my left arm open sliding home. In high school basketball, I was a center and one day a guy six-foot-six was guarding me. I'm six-foot-three now and was six-foot-two then, so I couldn't go over him; I had to outmaneuver him. I faked one way, then another, went up, and cracked my head into his teeth. I took twelve stitches in the top of my head.

I've had my appendix out and that was worth ten or twelve more stitches. When my younger brother and I were little kids, he hit me on the forehead with the butt of a cap gun—more stitches. A few years later, he was practicing his golf swing, and he caught me in the forehead with a golf club.

Three years ago, I tore up the muscles of my back in spring training. Two years ago, George Scott of the Red

Sox swung all the way around chasing a pitch, and his bat cracked my wrist. But I haven't missed many games since I got to the major leagues, and whenever I get hurt and have to face my teammates, I sort of feel embarrassed. Like I've done something that I'm not supposed to, or that I've let them down by getting hurt. I went down to the ballpark this morning before the guys left for Winter Haven and the big question was, "How long are you going to be out?" I told them what the doctor said, but I also said that *I* thought I'd be back a lot sooner than opening day.

Mayo seemed surprised to see me at the park. But there was no way, really, I could stay away.

March 22

I rode with the team to St. Petersburg, for our first exhibition game against our World Series opponents, the Cardinals. I still can't put on a uniform, but I was able to get in some eye exercise. That's right: eye exercise. Before the game, I stood behind the batting cage, directly behind the catcher, and kept watching the ball come in off the pitcher's hand. I picked up the ball fine every time. My eyes's going to be all right.

For me, the trip was a homecoming. I was born in Detroit and went to grade school there, but just as I was about to start high school, my father formed a corporation with some other men and bought a trailer park in St. Petersburg. We moved into a mobile home there, so he could manage the park, and I entered a small local Catholic high school.

I played high school football four years, as a quarterback and middle linebacker, and I played baseball for Bishop Barry High, too, as a catcher and pitcher. In the summers, I'd go back to Detroit, live with my grandparents, and play sandlot baseball. They played some of the best amateur baseball in America in Detroit, and

I played against a lot of guys who made it to the major leagues—guys like Willie Horton, Dave DeBusschere, Alex Johnson, and Dennis Ribant.

I'd started my baseball career around Detroit—as a shortstop in the Royal Oak Little League, where one of my opponents was Tom Hayden, who grew up to be a revolutionary and in college helped found the SDS, Students for a Democratic Society. Tom was a little guy, always arguing with the umpires and getting thrown out of games. Me, I was always a big kid and that was why, I guess, the Little League coach came up to me one day and said, "Hey, kid, would you like to put on the tools today?"

"The tools?"

"The tools of ignorance."

I didn't know what he meant.

"Catcher's equipment," he said.

As a catcher, I attracted the attention of major-league scouts while I was in high school. I also attracted some attention around St. Petersburg my senior year by being picked as second-team All-State quarterback behind George Mira, who now plays pro football, and by ending up third in my class academically. I was also president of the student council. In the past few years, when the Tigers have played in St. Petersburg, my high school has occasionally given the students a day off, so they can come down and cheer for me. Always, when they've done that, I've hit poorly and looked bad. Today I didn't have to worry about looking bad out on the field. I looked bad enough just standing there with that tape rolled around my face. Meet Bishop Barry's famous alumnus: the Monster Man.

March 23

We played the Cardinals again today, in Lakeland, and Mickey Lolich pitched against Bob Gibson, a replay of the seventh game of the World Series. The game was televised back to Detroit and St. Louis, and the crowd was a record for the Lakeland stadium. The game wasn't like most spring training exhibitions. There was some excitement in the air, some drama, for a change. It's tough to work up any incentive for winning an exhibition, but today both teams wanted to win.

We won a tight game, and Lolich pitched well. Mickey's been worrying that the new rule this year lowering the mound has been hurting his follow-through, but I was glad to see that he looked as effective as ever. I wasn't glad to be sitting out in the bullpen, in street clothes. I wanted to be in the game—or at least in the dugout where I could needle the guys a little, jab them about their mistakes.

A lot of people call me the leader of this club, and I'm a leader, I guess, because I'm not embarrassed to talk it up, to get on the guys when I see something going wrong or someone slacking off. But other guys are leaders, too, for other reasons. Cash—for his personality, his sense of humor. Dick McAuliffe, our second baseman—for his fire, his drive. Willie Horton—for his deeds, his bat.

The real leader of the team, probably, is Al Kaline, for his seniority and for his example, not for his words. He's not the oldest guy—Cash is a month or so older— but Al's been a Detroit Tiger for sixteen years, since he was eighteen years old, and it's almost impossible for me to imagine the Tigers without Al Kaline.

Al's quiet, and I've always wondered why he hasn't gone out of his way to talk it up more, to try to charge up the guys. The main reason, I'm sure, is his basic personality; Al's not a screamer or shaker away from the park either. There's merit in having the quiet dignity Al has. All the guys respect him. He'll stand in the outfield studying the game, always watching for that little thing that may someday turn a game around for our team. He knows all the hitters in the league, knows exactly where to play them. And he knows the pitchers, knows just what they throw and the situations in which they'll throw specific pitches.

And all the studying pays off for Al. Ever since he won the American League batting championship as a twenty-year-old—the youngest man ever to win it—he's been putting together a string of records that no other Tiger, except Ty Cobb, ever matched. Nobody moves with as much grace and makes fewer mistakes than Al Kaline. Out in right field and at bat, he's picture-perfect. His swing is fluid and quick-wristed, as beautiful as any in baseball. And in a crucial situation, he's doubly tough. he's The Man. Someday, when he's through playing, he'll probably be the manager here.

March 24

At 8:15 this morning, the doctor checked my nose, took out the cotton, and removed all the bandages and splints. It was beautiful to smell fresh air for the first time in a week.

It hurt, too. That first breath through my nose really stung the interior skin. I sniffed hard a few times, then I was all right.

The doctor told me to take it easy. He said the bones were knitting nicely, but the nose would be sore for a while. It would be all right for me to start running in about a week, he said, but now I had to be careful. "If you jar the nose," he said, "you're going to tear all those bones that have been mending."

I went out to the park and jogged a little. I played a little catch with one of the rookies, and I played some pepper, very carefully, making sure no ball took a bad hop and hit me in the nose. It felt great to have a uniform on.

The pay week ended today and the club made its first cut of the spring, sending about half a dozen guys to the minors. The club always cuts at the end of a pay week, just before the next week's meal money and living-allowance money—about $155 a man—is handed out.

Emotionally, this was an easy cut for the manager to make. He sent back only some young players, fellows who didn't really think they had chances for major-league jobs this year, but who are young enough and potentially good enough to be back sometime in the future. The tough cuts will come later. Guys with ten years in the major leagues will be told it's the end of the line. Kids with five good years in the minors will be told to be patient and come back again. Those cuts'll come, and they'll rip up some insides. They always do.

March 25

The club went to Tampa for a game against the Reds, and I stayed in Lakeland to work out. I swung at a few pitches, not too well, but my nose felt good and my vision was okay. My arms are still weak, but I expected that.

I feel everything inside me saying "Get back there, you can do it. Come on, push yourself now." It's that kind of feeling that makes you rush back and play on an injury that really hasn't healed. I once heard a baseball coach say, "Unless it's a 'do-or-die' situation where the pennant or World Series rides on one game, if a guy says he's ready after a minor injury, don't play him today, play him tomorrow. Just give him one more day because good athletes want to get back in there a little quicker than they ought to. One day too soon can mean another week or two on the bench with a reinjury."

So now my heart says go. But past experience has taught me to wait.

March 26

This evening we had a team party, our annual spring dinner. All the guys chipped in and the club picked up a piece of the cost, too. We got together with our wives at the Holiday Inn and after cocktails and dinner, there was some entertainment. Some of the veterans sang country songs, and the rookies wrote and sang a song about the veterans. Then we showed the promotional film about our 1968 success—Denny McLain winning his thirtieth game, our emotional last-minute victories, our World Series comeback. Most of the guys had already seen the film, but many of the wives hadn't, and we wanted to charge them up a little, too.

A woman can really help a man in this game—or hurt him. I know guys selling insurance and working in banks now who had the potential for very successful baseball careers. But their wives couldn't cope with the life—the weeks alone at home while the club was traveling, the struggling in the minors to work up to the big leagues, the emotional pressures brought home from the park on bad days. Not that these men aren't equally or more successful doing what they're doing now; it's just that inside, really, they wanted to play baseball. But they had some college education, as do about 30 percent of the guys who play in the major leagues these days, and they simply decided that it wasn't fair to their wives to stick to baseball when they could be doing well in another profession.

So we showed the film to psych up the wives a little bit, and when it ended Al Kaline made a short speech. Al's uncomfortable making speeches, but he is our elder statesman and he felt it was important to make this one. "We had a lot of fun last year," he said. "You saw it in those pictures. Let's make this year just like last year. And you girls have to be a help in this, too. So let's everybody in this room pull together and do it again."

Everybody walked out of the party with a real positive

feeling. Especially the wives, wearing the jewelry and the dresses we won in the World Series last year.

March 27

We've lost four of our last five exhibitions, and we've lost them badly. We're not pitching, we're not fielding, we're not hitting, we're not thinking.

Besides the fact that I can't play, three things are bothering me. First, Mayo hasn't chewed out the club. I think we'd all like him to sit down and yell at us—even if that's not his usual way.

Second, I see some friction developing between John Sain, our pitching coach, and Grover Resinger, our new third-base coach. John believes that the less pressure you put on a pitcher the better he's going to do; Grover believes in being tough and squawking at guys all the time. Grover's been talking to some of the guys about how he disagrees with Sain's methods, how he thinks Sain is too easygoing. When John joined us in 1967, it took a lot of us time to adjust to his ways; I imagine Grover'll get used to them, too.

Third, we're hurting at shortstop. We had a great defensive shortstop last year, Ray Oyler, who was taken away from us by Seattle in the expansion draft. Tommy Matchick and Dick Tracewski have been playing short for us during spring training, but they're basically utility men; the guy who played short in the World Series, Mickey Stanley, has had a bad arm.

Mickey's regular position is center field—he's one of the best, if not the best center fielder in baseball—but he's also the best all-round athlete we've got. He's a high-strung guy, very aggressive, and I think he hurt his arm early this spring by trying to learn instantly everything there is to learn about playing shortstop. He's accustomed to throwing mainly overhand from the outfield, but at shortstop he has to throw sidearm and three-quarter-arm a great deal because you can't take as much time getting rid of the ball. He was out there, taking two hundred, three hundred balls a day and slinging them to first with muscles he'd never used in center field. I think Mickey'll be our shortstop, and I think he'll do a fine job, but we're going to suffer if his arm doesn't heal soon. He's got to learn the job in spring training, not during league games.

We lost another good man to Seattle—Wayne Comer, a reserve outfielder. But a rookie, Ron Woods, who batted .292 for Toledo last year and is the fastest man on our squad, looks like he'll win that job. Two other rookies, Mike Kilkenny and Fred Scherman, have been pitching well and might win jobs, too; both of them are left-handers and even last season we needed left-handed relief pitching. Another new man who's looked good is Dick "The Monster" Radatz, who's had a few bad seasons lately, but once, with the Boston Red Sox, was the best relief pitcher in baseball.

A major-league team can carry only twenty-five players on its roster during the season and eleven of them at the most will be pitchers. It appears now that our top four starting pitchers will be the same as last year—McLain, Lolich, Earl Wilson, and my road roommate, Joe Sparma —and that the others will be John Hiller, who won nine games for us last season; Pat Dobson, who was number one in our bullpen; Kilkenny, Scherman, Radatz, Don McMahon, and Fred Lasher.

The infield, I guess, will be Cash at first, McAuliffe at second, and Don Wert at third—all regulars in 1968— plus Stanley at short, and Matchick, Tracewski, and a rookie, Dave Campbell, in reserve. Kaline, Horton, and Northrup will be the outfielders, with Gates Brown and Woods behind them. The catchers, once again, will be me and Jim Price.

That's pennant-winning personnel; now one of these days we'd better start playing pennant-winning ball.

March 28

I can tell I'm feeling good again: I'm mad at myself. I went down to the bullpen, caught with a mask on just to get used to it, and felt fine. Then I took batting practice and hit the ball well. But when I got a chance to pinch-hit in the game, I popped up. That teed me off. I shouldn't have popped that ball up.

All through my career, I've literally hated myself for failure. One of these days I'm going to find a manager who's harder on me than I am on myself. But so far I haven't met him.

I've always been restless, always wanted to do a lot of things, play all the notes on the scale. My senior year in high school, I was offered college scholarships by Georgia Tech, Auburn, Florida, Florida State, Miami, Western Michigan, Michigan, West Point, the Naval Academy, dozens of other schools. As a Catholic and a football player, I wanted to go to Notre Dame, but I wanted to play both baseball and football, and when Notre Dame offered me a scholarship, I was told, "You want to skip spring football practice and play baseball? Sure you can— if you're an All-American in football your sophomore year."

I decided to go to Western Michigan.

A friend of mine from sandlot ball, Dick Honig, also accepted a scholarship to Western Michigan and we drove up together for preregistration. When we got to Western Michigan, I looked at Dick and said, "You know, I went to a small high school and I was always getting beat by numbers. I think I'm going to leave right now and take a scholarship at the University of Michigan." Michigan was about an hour back down the turnpike.

"I'll ride with you," he said. We drove down to Ann Arbor, and both of us signed in.

Don Lund, the Michigan baseball coach, gave me a

scholarship. I wasn't sure I was good enough to play football at Michigan—I was a little awed by all those high-
school All-Americans—but after watching the freshmen
practice one day, I decided I had to find out for myself
exactly how good they were. They had seventeen
quarterbacks and I would have been the eighteenth, but
I saw that some of the ends could hardly catch the ball.
I decided to try out as an end. I made the team, and then,
as a sophomore, played more minutes than any other end
on the varsity.

In baseball my sophomore year, I batted .585, a Big
Ten record, and set other records for home runs and runs
batted in. The major-league bonus offers, which had
gone up to $35,000 when I graduated from high school,
now went shooting up into six figures. It was a lot of
money, and my family had never been rich.

I decided to turn pro. I signed with the Tigers for a
total of $125,000.

Detroit's wasn't the highest offer, but I took it for three
reasons. One, the package was good enough; two, I was
from Detroit; and three, because the Tigers had no out-
standing catcher, I figured I could get to the majors pretty
quick. I put most of my bonus money into stocks, promised myself I'd get my degree from Michigan during the
off-season (which I have, in liberal arts), and reported
in 1961 to the Tigers' Northern League farm team,
Duluth-Superior. I played thirty games for Duluth-
Superior and batted almost .350. I was on my way.

Two years later, I was in the big leagues for good. As
a rookie, I batted .243; the next year I hit .300 with eighty
runs batted in. I had two poor seasons after that, but in
1967 Mayo Smith became our manager and brought
along Wally Moses as batting coach. Wally moved me
closer to the plate and told me to use my front arm more
for bat speed and power; my batting average went up
from .234 to .282, my RBIs increased from forty-six to
seventy-four, and my home runs from twelve to twenty.

One year later, I was a world champion. I like the way that sounds.

March 30

At church for Palm Sunday services this morning, the priest was fighting a losing battle for my attention. All during his sermon, I kept thinking of my decision not to try to play in a game until Tuesday. All I could think was: "Why not today?"

Why not? When my wife and daughters dropped me off at the park, I went to the equipment man and got my catcher's mask. I stuck it on my head, then whipped it off. It didn't bother me as it brushed past my nose. I put it on again and gave myself a couple of good whacks on the top of my mask. No pain.

With the mask on, I walked into the manager's office. "Hey, Skip," I said, "take a look at this." I smacked myself on the mask a couple more times. "Doesn't bother me," I said. "Why wait until Tuesday? Let me play today."

"You sure?" Mayo said. The way the team's been playing, he needed some good news.

"Yeah."

Mayo popped out of his chair and walked toward me. I didn't know what he had in mind. Without a word, he reached out and whacked me hard across the mask. "Sure it doesn't hurt?" he said.

"Nope."

"Okay. Let's try it."

I played six innings, and the only time I had any pain was when I ripped off the mask quickly to go after pop-ups. When I got hom , my wife said, "When you said good-bye outside the c - I knew you had something on your mind. You had th funny look on your face, and I just knew you were going to play today."

I liked that. It's nice to know your wife can read your feelings.

April 1

I'm playing completely naturally again, except for a tendency to shy away from hard contact on plays at the plate. Usually, I have a lot of fun and pride in blocking the plate. That's the closest an old football player can come to making baseball a contact sport.

April 2

Today is what we call "Freedom Day." The wives and kids went home to Detroit. For the next week we can make that final push toward the season without worrying about taking the kids to school or getting home in time to set up the barbecue after the game.

April 3

After we came in from batting practice, the coaches began walking over to certain guys, one at a time, to say, "Hey, Mayo wants to talk to you." Mayo was making the final cuts, getting the roster down to twenty-five, and in his office he was telling guys that they were being let go.

The toughest job a manager has is calling a guy into the office to let him know he's been released, traded, or sent down to the minor leagues. I've only been called in once—in 1962. But I was twenty years old, in my first spring training; I hadn't expected to stay with the Tigers. I've never had the agonizing experience of being called in and dropped when I thought, finally, after years of success in the minors, I was going to get a chance in the majors. And I've never been told that, after years in the majors, I was through. I guess I've still got that to look forward to.

Two of the pitchers cut yesterday have been in the majors more than ten years each—Roy Face and John Wyatt. Wyatt was bitter and, I think, rightfully so. He pitched well for us last season and just wasn't given much of a chance in spring training to prove he still was good. Dick Radatz got most of the relief work in the spring, and Dick was told today that he'd made the club.

Wayne Redmond, a reserve outfielder, was cut, which meant that Ron Woods made the team. Ron's about the same age as I am, but he's been playing in the minor leagues for eight years. He's never been up to bat even once in a big-league game. When I saw him after the cuts today, his eyes were wet. "Congratulations," I said.

"This is the happiest day of my life," he said. His voice was all choked up.

"The easy part's over now," I said. "The hard part's in front of you."

"Maybe this was the easy part for you," he said, "but it was the hard part for me. I've been at this game for eight years, and wasn't sure if I ever was going to make it. I'm a little guy, and you're a big guy, and they always look at the big guys first. As far as I'm concerned, the hard part's behind me. I'm just happy to be here."

I led Ron to the Gatorade—I'd spiked the soft drink with a fifth and a half of vodka—and pretty soon he was laughing and I was laughing, and everybody was laughing.

Everybody except the guys who got cut.

April 5

In Montgomery, Alabama, today, before our exhibition game was rained out, I noticed our batboy had on a uniform so tattered and sewn you couldn't figure out where the patches began and the material ended.

"Hey, kid," I said to the batboy. "Where'd you get that uniform?"

"Used to be Ronnie Woods'," the kid said. "He was my favorite player when he was here two years ago."

"Ron," I said, "you must've had a tough season. You must've been sliding a whole lot because those britches look like they've been on the ground and torn up a few times."

Ronnie smiled. "When you're in the minor leagues," he said, "you're just happy they have a uniform for you in the locker room. You don't worry about what it looks like. It's not the big leagues."

Ron's right. I remember my days in the minors, the hot days in the dingy locker rooms of the South Atlantic League. I remember especially one day, a Sunday, when I was playing in Columbia, South Carolina, and my folks came to watch me play for the first time as a pro.

The temperature was 113 degrees in the shade, and we were in the sun, and I caught both games of a double-header. We lost both games by one run, and afterward, in our locker room, set under the wooden stands, our manager lectured for an hour and a half.

The locker room was barely big enough for ten guys, and there must've been thirty of us in there. We'd been on the road for ten days, and our uniforms hadn't been cleaned for ten days. I thought I'd die in there; the sweat literally poured off me. When the meeting finally ended, and I came out in my uniform stained by today's sweat and yesterday's mud to say good-bye to my folks, they said good-bye in a hurry.

Just one whiff of the minor-league life was enough for them.

April 6

We played our final exhibition game today, against the Cincinnati Reds, and we lost it. We finished the spring with nine victories and seventeen defeats, our worst pre-season record in seven years. Our chief rivals, the Baltimore Orioles, won nineteen exhibitions and lost only five. Aside from the record, we sure didn't look much like world champions. We've been playing in a daze, like we expected to win just on our reputation.

One of our main problems has been Denny McLain, but I'm not too worried about him. Denny can turn on his valve a little differently from the rest of us. He hasn't even been with us for five days. He's been home nursing a sore shoulder, but he says he'll be ready on opening day. I've learned not to doubt Denny; over the years, he's made me a believer.

Denny's a tough guy to understand. His concentration wanders a lot when he's on the mound, and off the mound *he* wanders a lot—running off after games to play the organ in nightclubs, flying around in his plane, looking after all his businesses. I've never had real good rapport with Denny. He likes to fight with me about strategy, and when things aren't going well for him he likes to break things and yell at the fans and the other players.

I've never had as much trouble communicating with any other pitcher as I've had with Denny. But, at the same time, I've never caught a better pitcher in my life. When Denny goes out there and puts his mind to it, he's the best pitcher in the world.

After the game today, I sat in the locker room a long time, the way I like to, letting everything inside me calm down. Pretty soon, everyone cleared out, except me and Grover Resinger, our new third-base and infield coach, and Grover and I started talking about the coming season.

"You know," Grover said, "my players are going to be okay"—he meant the infielders—"but there's no way we can win this summer because our pitchers just aren't in shape."

Grover shook his head. He used to train fighters, and he's a physical-fitness bug, and he said he was very upset with John Sain, our pitching coach, for not putting the pitchers through much physical training. "We're going to hit," Grover said, "and Mickey Stanley will do the job at shortstop. But what I see in our pitchers just doesn't show me anything."

I was a little worried by what I was hearing. I could understand Grover—he's a pusher, a driver, just like I am—but I also knew how good Sain is. He's had more success than any other pitching coach I've ever seen. His methods may be unorthodox—he doesn't believe in much running or exercising for his pitchers—but he gets results.

Grover's remarks disturbed me, but I talked calmly to him. "I hope you don't really feel that way, Grover," I said, "because I think we can win. We can all win—the pitchers, the infielders, the outfielders, everybody."

I realized that Grover wasn't really down on the ball club, not even down on the pitching staff. He just couldn't see how a bunch of pitchers could get in shape without running.

Afterward, the more I thought about what Grover said, the more it worried me. As a catcher, I'm sort of in the middle; I'm close to the pitchers, naturally, because I catch them, and I'm close to the "other players" because I'm a hitter, too. It's part of my job to keep the club together, to keep everyone pulling together, to prevent splits. Grover's a good coach—a hard worker, an intelligent baseball man—but I'm afraid his attitude toward Sain and the pitchers might cause undercurrents in this club.

The way we've been playing, we can't afford undercurrents. Any kind of split—the infielders versus the pitchers, the hitters versus the pitchers—could kill our chances of repeating as world champions.

April 7

The local press—you know, the guys who said they'd never give up on the Tigers again—have already written us off. We haven't played our first game, and they say we're not going to win the pennant. Well, I think we're going to win.

Mayo does, too. "We had a bad spring," he told us at a meeting this morning, "but that's all behind us now. We've got a season here in front of us. We can win. We've got a good club. All we've got to do is start paying attention to basic fundamentals from here on in." He went over his rules, telling us that on road trips every player would travel with the team, that there would be absolutely no exceptions. He said that on the road, curfew was midnight after day games, and two-and-a-half hours after the bus got back to the hotel following a night game. There'd be a $100 fine for breaking curfew, he said, but he wasn't going to be real strict. "I expect you to act like men," he said.

Mayo talked to us for just a few minutes, then we had a light workout. I went out to the outfield where Grover was supervising the running. "You know, what you said yesterday has really been bothering me," I told him. "I'm in the middle of the pitchers and the other guys, and it's my job to speak up now because I think you're going to create a problem. If you've got some meaningful suggestions, speak to John or the manager. Sain's got a way about him. It may not be the way you like, but he's had some great success."

I looked at Grover and I said, "You know, if you don't think we can win, then you ought not to be here."

"No," Grover said. "I didn't want to give you the impression I didn't think we could win. I'm sorry I gave you that impression. I think we've got a good chance to win. It's just that I've seen things here that have been different from anything I've ever seen. But I like the people on this club. I'll get used to it. And I think we're gonna win. I'm sure of it."

I hope he means it—and I hope he's right.

I'm going to have trouble sleeping tonight. I always do the night before opening day. All my plans, my hopes are going to be running through my mind. Personally, I hope I stay free from injury. I've been lucky the past two years; I've been able to play more than 150 games a season. Also, I'd like to increase my RBIs, drive in more than eighty-five runs, and bat maybe .280 or .285 with twenty-five or so home runs. But I'll give up ten home runs and twenty RBIs and thirty points off my batting average—hell, I'm even willing to accept another broken nose or two—just as long as I get that feeling again I got last October.

2

GUESS
WHO
WON?

April 8

Before the opening game today in Detroit, Bowie Kuhn, the commissioner of baseball, gave us our World Series rings, something a lot of us have dreamed about for a long time. I don't think any of us felt quite so proud as Al Kaline. He'd waited so long, sixteen years to play in his first World Series, sixteen years to win a world championship. When he received his ring from the commissioner at home plate, he held it high in the air all the way back to the dugout so that the whole crowd could see it.

"These rings," Al said, as he came into the dugout, "that's what we're shooting for in '69." For Al, that was a pretty big speech.

Just before we took the field, Norm Cash came running over to Mayo Smith. All last year, we'd begun each inning by tossing a special ball around the infield—a ball colored red and blue with a marking pencil. Somehow, we'd forgotten about that ball all spring, and today Norm yelled to Mayo, who's really a superstitious guy, "Hey, Skip, you want the colored infield ball?"

Mayo's eyes lit up, as if all of a sudden he knew the reason for our bad spring. "Hey, oh, yeah," he said. "I'd forgotten about that." And he ran to the telephone and called the clubhouse and had the trainer mark up a ball and bring it right out. Mayo's eyes were sparkling. "We gotta have that," he said.

Maybe there's something to all those superstitions.

Denny McLain rejoined us today. He pitched a three-hitter, just like the old days, and we beat Cleveland, 6-2.

April 10

When I have a bad day, I don't read the newspapers. I let my wife screen them for me. But tomorrow I'm definitely going to be reading the papers. I hit a grand-slam home run today off Sam McDowell, added a double and another home run, and drove in five runs. We won easily. If I can keep this up, I'll hit 162 home runs this year.

April 11

My wife made me eat exactly the same breakfast this morning that I ate yesterday. My neighbor sent over the exact same kind of brownies she'd sent over yesterday morning. My stockbroker's wife called to remind me that I'd had mushroom sauce with her spaghetti the other night. And my brother-in-law called to congratulate me on the four-leaf clover he'd just given me. Everyone was taking credit for my great game yesterday.

Then the Yankees beat us this afternoon and stole five bases in five attempts against me. I guess I'll have to change my diet and my stockbroker tomorrow.

April 12

Mel Stottlemyre of the Yankees pitched a one-hitter today and beat us and Denny McLain. Jim Northrup got our only hit. We had two one-hitters pitched against us last year, and both times Jim got the hit. "Don't worry," he kept saying all spring. "No one's going to throw any no-hitters against us 'cause I'm going to break them up." We all ought to go up to the plate with that attitude.

Our record is 2-2, even .500. That's the way we measure our progress, the number of games over .500 or under .500. To win our division, I figure we're going to have to be about twenty-eight games over .500. That'd give us a record of 95-67, a percentage of about .580. (We were 103-59 last year, a percentage of .636, but we could've won at .580; the second-place Orioles finished only twenty games over .500.)

We have to get a good jump on .500 right now, when it's toughest, when all the teams are still confident. If we can get twelve or fourteen games over .500 by the All-Star break in July, we'll be in pretty good shape. In August, the teams that are out of contention have a lot less spirit and unity than they've got in April; they're easier to beat then.

April 14

We started our first road trip today. My wife is always sad when we leave town, and I don't blame her. She's got to be both mother and father for eleven days. It's tough.

Baseball players are gone from their families for longer extended periods than any other professional athletes. Pro golfers are always on the road, I guess, but their families can travel with them. Not ours. I was playing baseball before I got married, so when Pat married me, she knew she was getting two things—me and baseball. She's learned to cope with both of us pretty well.

There's nothing like your first day on the road to let you know the season has really started. I don't have to worry about phone calls or yard work or bills or the kids. I wake up, read the newspaper, eat breakfast, and just think about baseball, nothing else.

For the last two or three years, I've hit better on the road than at home. Al Kaline's the same way. Al says it's much easier to concentrate on the road, and I agree. To me, concentration's about 75 percent of the game—thinking, right from the minute you get up, about the opposing team, its tendencies in certain situations, the pitches the man you're going to face likes to throw.

On the other hand, road trips can be the downfall of a baseball player. With the night games and the constant pressure, nobody gets to sleep early every night. But the pros know enough to get their rest when they need it, and they come ready to play every day, no matter how they feel, even if they've been up too late, even if the cards or the women have been bad, even if they've had too much to drink.

Some of the guys occasionally boost their energy with what we call "greenies"—pep pills, Benzedrine, something like that, a little false energy. The trouble is that if you get too dependent on these instant pick-me-ups, they can shorten your career. Our manager's definitely opposed to the use of pills, and our trainer'll confiscate any he finds.

Jim Campbell, our general manager, once told me that if he ever heard of any of our guys using these pills, he'd take some very strict action, because he feels they have no part in the game. Most of the players on the team agree with him.

April 15

We played the Indians in Cleveland today, and I swear there couldn't have been more than seven hundred people in the stands. It was depressing, playing in a big, empty stadium. Probably the toughest thing in baseball is getting yourself up emotionally day after day after day. At least football players have six days to rebuilt emotionally for each game, but we don't. Mayo kept yelling at us today, "Push, push, you gotta push," but we just couldn't get charged up.

Emmett Ashford was the umpire behind home plate today. He's a character, always jumping around, and he's great to give a little life to a one-sided game. But in a close game, his antics can be awfully distracting. We had a close game today—tied, 2-2, going into the eighth inning—and both sides had been complaining about some of his calls.

In the eighth, Ashford called Norm Cash out on a questionable curve, and Norman delivered a pretty good outburst. I was in the on-deck circle, and I heard Ashford warn Norm he'd better be quiet. Norm stopped talking, then suddenly yelled, "That's the *second* pitch you missed on me." For emphasis, Norm stuck up two fingers, one for each pitch missed.

Ashford, who didn't hear what Norm said, thought he was seeing an obscene gesture. He threw Norm out of the game.

The Indians who'd lost their first five games of the year, eventually beat us in the tenth inning, and José Cardenal, who'd knocked in the winning run, ran to their dugout with one finger raised over his head. Someone asked Cardenal if that was a Latin-American victory sign, and he said, "No, that's our number of wins. I'm going to count off each one all year." The way the Indians have been playing, Jose may not need too many fingers.

Afterward, when Ashford found out what Cash had said, the umpire was a little embarrassed. Norm was philosophical about the whole thing. Dave Campbell, who'd replaced him at first base, had made a great defensive play to send the game into extra innings. Norm told the rest of us that if Ashford hadn't kicked him out, he wouldn't have been able to make that play, we would've lost the game in nine innings, and we all would have gotten out of the ball park an inning earlier. By not hearing Norman, all Ashford did was shorten our cocktail hour.

April 17

We beat the Indians today—we're two games over .500 now—then flew into New York this evening. We did a lot of singing on the plane and on the bus—Mickey Lolich carries some Johnny Cash tapes with him, and we just sing along with Johnny—and we did our usual agitating, a lot of good, clean fun. Pat Dobson was one target. He'd given up a home run in the ninth inning to Tony Horton of the Indians, and Jim Northrup started needling Pat, "What were you trying to do with that fast ball to Horton? Kill a perch in Lake Erie?" The lake starts just beyond the left-field fence, and Horton had hit the ball over the fence.

Most of the time on planes and in buses, we laugh and sing and kid, but once in a while the conversation gets pretty risque, pretty wild. We must reach our peak during the bus rides in New York, when we're driving up Madison Avenue at rush hour on the way to a night game at Yankee Stadium. We pass some of the weirdest-looking women, weirdest-looking couples, and weirdest-looking dogs, and we average Midwestern boys just have to react to things like that. We react pretty strongly. If you've got virgin ears, you better stay off a baseball team's bus.

Once last year, on a trip to New York, a girl reporter took a bus ride with us, and most of the guys didn't know she was aboard. John Sain sat next to her and kept talking all the way, trying to drown out the songs and comments in the background, but he didn't succeed too well. The reporter ended up writing a dandy little column about us. She embarrassed us even more than we'd embarrassed her.

April 21

We moved into Washington today, nursing our wounds. Four days in New York didn't hurt us much on the field —we split two games—but it killed us in the wallet. I had orange juice and a sweet roll for breakfast one morning and paid $1.62. I had a hamburger, tossed salad and two Cokes sent to my room at the Hotel Roosevelt—$7.62. That's a little rough on us country boys.

Dick Radatz was saying on the bus today that the four days in New York hit him so hard he couldn't even buy a low-cut dress for a hummingbird. He was so broke, he said, he had toothpicks for breakfast.

The Monster—he's six-foot-seven—can be a funny man. He told us that when he's had a rough road trip, financially, he gets off the plane, kisses his wife hello, then reaches for his wallet. Gone. He tells his wife it must've been stolen. About three days later, Radatz said, he mails his wallet to his home—all his credit cards and papers included, but no money—with a typewritten note signed by an imaginary man, explaining that he found Mr. Radatz's wallet and thought he'd like to have it back. Mr. Radatz promptly sends the imaginary man two tickets to a ball game, out of deep gratitude, and his wife tells him how lucky he is to have his wallet back.

A few of the guys were riding Fred Lasher, another one of our relief pitchers. Fred's not quite an Aristotle Onassis; we get $15-a-day meal money, and I suspect Fred sends half of his home. We call him Mr. Ed sometimes, because he looks, and acts, a little like that talking horse from the old television show.

"Hey, Lash," somebody yelled, "I hear you managed to save some money on this trip."

"Naw," he said. "Spent it all."

"Sure you did, Lash," somebody else said. "Hay's pretty expensive in New York."

Everything's pretty expensive in New York. Matter of fact, I think somebody stole my wallet there.

My roommate, Joe Sparma, pitched tonight, his first start of the season. He had an off-year in 1968—he dropped from sixteen victories in 1967 to ten last year—and once, when Mayo pulled him out of a game in the first inning, he and the manager had a few words. They haven't gotten along too well since, and Joe was beginning to suspect he'd never get a start. He got it tonight, and he shut out the Senators. He looks like he's going to be our fourth starting pitcher.

Joe's got all the physical equipment to be a consistent winner, but he has to work on his temper. A couple of guys sitting behind our dugout tonight were riding him, and he made the mistake of listening to them. "Bum," they kept yelling. "You'd be out of there if you didn't have good defensive plays behind you."

In the eighth inning, Dick McAuliffe got us out of trouble with a great play at second base, and one of the needlers hollered, "You're still a bum. The defense is saving you."

"That's what they get paid for," Joe snapped back.

Joe's got to learn not to answer the hecklers back. The best way to put them down is just not to say anything.

April 22

I got a great phone call this morning—a $500 phone call from an advertising agency in Detroit. I did a commercial for the National Bank of Detroit last year, and they want to use the commercial again this year. The guy who called said I'd get $500 for the rights to use the same commercial. No new filming. No work. Just collect. I guess that makes up for the hamburger I got from room service in New York.

Before the game tonight, I bumped into the new Washington manager, my boyhood idol, Ted Williams. In 1961, when I was a sophomore at the University of Michigan and thinking about turning pro, the Boston Red Sox sent Williams to my house to talk to me for a few minutes. I saw him again at an All-Star game a couple of years ago and said hello and talked to him about hitting, but I was sure he didn't remember me at all. Then, tonight, he came up to me by the batting cage and said, "Hey, kid, how you doing? You've come a long way since I saw you at your house in Detroit."

It made me feel damn good, Ted Williams remembering me. I was just about at a loss for words. I mumbled something like, "Well, yes, it has been a long grind," but I was just happy for the recognition. I know I was trying extra hard tonight to impress Williams. So was Kaline. Al was swinging the bat as if he were saying, "Look, here's another great hitter."

We staged a Tiger Finish tonight, coming from behind for the second time in three days to win a game. We scored three runs in the ninth inning and won, 4-2. We're 8-4 now, four games over .500, and I think we're starting to move.

We'd better be. We go into Baltimore tomorrow, and the Orioles are leading our division. They're 11-5, a game in front of us, but if we win tomorrow night, we climb into first place. That's the only place to be.

April 23

Before the game in Baltimore today, we visited the Naval Academy at Annapolis and when they showed us their central computer, Denny McLain, who was going to open the series for us, said, "Ask it if I should pitch tonight."

The machine said, "No." Mayo looked over his shoulder at Earl Wilson and said, "You're pitching tonight." We laughed.

We weren't laughing later. The machine was right.

We were ahead, 2-0, in the bottom of the second inning, and Mark Belanger, the Oriole shortstop, hit a two-run homer. In the bottom of the tenth, Belanger singled in another run and Baltimore beat Denny, 3-2.

Belanger is a skinny guy, probably the least likely man on the field to hit a home run. He's not too likely to hit a single, either. He batted only .208 last year.

I've been telling Denny for a couple of years now that he has a tendency to concentrate only on the big hitters in the lineup and then relax on the seventh, eighth, and ninth hitters. He gets in trouble with the little guys, but no matter how much I ride his butt, he doesn't change. The last thing he and I talked about before the game was not to let the little guys get on base.

"That's the most embarrassing moment of my life," Denny said, after Belanger's home run. He was almost grinning.

He didn't have anything funny to say after Belanger's single.

April 24

Baltimore beat us again today. We're only two games over .500, and they're eight games over. There's no question now: Baltimore's the team we have to beat. Their pitching's strong, Frank Robinson's healthy and, with two straight victories over us, their morale is high. We've got to start hitting.

April 25

The real name of this game is pack and repack. I didn't get home to bed till three o'clock this morning.

In the past twelve days, I've been in five different towns, and I've packed five times and unpacked five times.

I get four new suits each season, and for seven months, they go in and out of a suitcase. All I've got at the end are four suits I can give to a relief agency.

I've got to say one thing for baseball: it makes you an expert traveler. You learn little tricks, like how to get wrinkles out of a suit by hanging it in the bathroom and turning on the hot water in the shower full blast; it's do-it-yourself steam pressing. I wonder how many University of Michigan liberal arts graduates know that?

Baseball also teaches you to get by without much sleep. My daughters woke me up at seven this morning: "Hey, dad"—they recognized me; you always wonder if they will—"you got to come see our neat new boat in the garage." Kids don't understand that four hours of sleep just hasn't got it.

I went out to the park at five o'clock. And about half an hour before game time, Mickey Lolich got in from two weeks of Air National Guard duty. He put on his uniform and went right out to pitch against Boston. Mickey did well, too, except for a couple of mistakes—back-to-back home runs—in the middle innings. When you pitch for the new Hitless Wonders, you can't do that and expect to win.

We lost, the first defeat for Mickey in nine decisions, going back through his three World Series victories. I made certain to get into the locker room with Mickey and talk to him quick because he gets depressed easily.

"Mick," I said, "I don't want you to be experimenting just because you got beat tonight."

Lolich has a habit of doing this; if one game isn't a success he wants to change his whole style of pitching. I told him he had pretty good stuff and not to make any changes. I said the warm air helped give distance to some of the Red Sox hits, and not to worry about it. I think I got through to him. I hope so. Mickey's got a lot of pride and a lot of guts, but not all the confidence in the world. He always seems to be trying to prove things to himself, racing around on motorcycles, for example, and in souped-up cars.

I think if I ever won three World Series games, I wouldn't have to prove anything any more.

April 26

We were on national television today, the first time since the World Series, and Mickey Mantle was doing the pregame show. During batting practice, I sat in the dugout for a while with Mickey, and Kaline saw us and came by. "Al," Mickey said, "you don't realize how easy this game is until you get up in that broadcasting booth."

It is easy for Mickey now. He doesn't have to show up for every national TV game, so he picks out the ones in cities he likes. He'll go to the West Coast, he told us, and Montreal, and Minneapolis. "Billy Martin's the manager up there," he said, "and that might be interesting." He doesn't even have to stay around for the game. When he was out in San Diego, on his first job, he flew out right after his pregame show and by the third inning was in Las Vegas.

"How long do I get on the air today?" he asked one of the directors.

"Oh, about three and a half minutes," the director said.

"You know, I fly all the way up here from Dallas," Mickey said, "and if that's all you're going to use me, I don't know if it's worth my while."

"Well, if you ever learned to talk," the director said, "you could do more. But with that accent of yours, hell, we can't expect people to put up with that for more than three and a half minutes."

Norm Cash came by then, and he and Mickey started talking, two old country boys going at it, and they both sounded like they had a mouthful of mush.

We played a ball game, too. Carl Yastrzemski hit a grandslam home run for Boston, and we had our fourth straight defeat. We're no games over .500 now. Where are the Tiger Finishes?

April 27

Denny McLain broke our losing streak. He really did pitch. Not throw. Pitch. You expect a pitcher to be sharp, to have his good fast ball, maybe three times out of five. The rest of the time, he has to finess it; he has to *pitch*. McLain realized early today that he didn't have his best hard stuff. After he warmed up, he came back to the bench and said, "Hey, let's go, you guys. I'm going to go as hard as I can for as long as I can. Then Mayo better get somebody to pick me up for the other eight and two-third innings."

Then Denny went out and adjusted—he used his breaking ball and mixed his pitches—and we beat Boston. Denny and I got along a little better than usual; we were thinking along the same lines. I hope that keeps up.

Our scrubbies—the substitutes—played an important part in the win, too. Tommy Matchick played third base, and it looks as if he's going to replace Don Wert as a starter for a while. Dick Tracewski filled in for McAuliffe at second, and Ron Woods, who hadn't been swinging well at all, got a chance to pinch-hit and knocked in two runs with his first major-league hit.

Ronny's locker is next to mine and pretty often, because the writers like to talk to the catcher, he gets crowded out of his cubicle. We were sipping beers when the writers came by today, and when Ron started to move away, I said, "They don't want to talk to me."

He looked around and said, "Hey, you guys want to talk to *me?*"

It really helps to have the second line come in and do a job because it not only perks them up, it perks up the regulars. We know we're going to have to depend on these people during the season. Our scrubbies have great unity. They have their own code of ethics—things like how many swings they're allowed to take in batting practice, who pitches batting practice. They even have a formal "Scrubbie Oath": "On my honor, I will do my duty, when called upon, to perform up to my capability, to pull and cheer for the scrubbies and when needed give a few words of kindness or a pat on the back to fellow scrubbies." They've also printed up a list of "Scrubbie No-nos": A scrubbie cannot "yell or holler at scrubbie pitcher," "show up scrubbie pitcher by means of obscene gestures," or "brown-nose." If you are the scrubbie picked to pitch batting practice, "you will say, 'It is my pleasure, sir;'" you will not complain. A scrubbie gets fined a dollar for committing a "no-no" and also for "failure to wish good luck to a fellow scrubbie who gets a start." Both the "Scrubbie Oath" and the list of "Scrubbie No-nos" are signed, "Gates Brown, The Enforcer, and Jim Price, The Big Guy." Gates is massive and logically enough, The Enforcer. Price is twenty-five pounds lighter than Gates, even fifteen pounds lighter than me, and no one's been able to figure out why he's The Big Guy.

April 28

It takes me about twenty minutes to drive from my home to the ball park and when I'm alone, I concentrate so hard on the game, I get there as if on automatic pilot. Kaline's the same way. "You know, sometimes when I'm driving to the ball park I don't even remember seeing the exit sign," Al's told me. "I'm concentrating on the road, but my thoughts aren't involved with the mechanical operation of the car. I'm thinking about what to do on the field."

An outfielder, like Al, basically thinks about offense; nine times out of ten, his thoughts are on who's pitching for the other team and how that pitcher works against him. But a catcher has different problems. My thoughts are mostly about our pitcher—what he likes to do against the club we're playing—and about the opposing hitters. I decide which guys I don't want to beat me. For instance, I check the papers over the past few days to see which hitters are hot to make certain we pitch carefully to those guys. Some guys are always a threat. Like, we're playing Washington now, and we don't want Frank Howard to beat us. Whenever he comes up and we have an opportunity to pitch around him—throw to the corners and a little bit outside, say, even at the risk of walking him— we'll do it. We'll take our chances on throwing in the strike zone to the next batter. If the man behind Howard beats us, okay. The odds on him doing it are less than the odds on Howard doing it.

People often complain that catchers ought to be better hitters. We could be, if we spent 90 percent of our time thinking about offense, like an outfielder or infielder. But every good catcher has to concentrate on defense.

My thinking did a lot of good tonight. Frank Howard didn't beat us. The man behind him—Hank Allen—did. Allen drove in four runs, and we sank back to .500.

April 29

Mickey Stanley woke up this morning with a strep throat, and his wife told him not to go to the park. She was worrying about his health, but Mickey was worrying more about the team. He came, he played, and he won the game with a bases-loaded double in the ninth—a Tiger Finish, at last.

Dick Radatz got the win over Washington, his first as a Tiger. The general manager, Jim Campbell, hasn't made up his mind yet about keeping Radatz, and he asked me to keep him posted on Dick's control and fast ball. I'll be able to tell Campbell tomorrow that Radatz looked good, that he was throwing the way he did back when he played for Boston.

I didn't look so good. I think I've had three hits in a week. It's something like what I went through last year in the World Series. They gave out pay checks yesterday, and when the man came with mine, I didn't even look at him. I put my hand out behind my back. I felt like I was stealing.

April 30

I spent a lot of time tonight hitting against Iron Mike, the pitching machine. I've been out early three days in a row now, trying to snap my slump. It's rough, being out there with Wally Moses, our batting instructor, watching. You're hitting and hitting for forty minutes and you hear that squeaky little voice coming from the side of the cage and you'd just like to turn and tell him to shut up; but you don't, for one good reason: Wally knows what he's talking about.

Wally's on me now to keep my weight on the back foot when I stride—not to shift my weight and glide into the ball, but just to step into it. He's trying to get me to use my left hand a whole lot more to get the bat out in front. Well, the ideas he's talking about are tremendous, but when he keeps pounding them into you, over and over, sometimes you suspect that he doesn't give the hitter credit for any intelligence. Still, he's got a great record for helping hitters. I know he's helped me.

The trouble with being in a slump and practicing so hard is that when you're in a game, you start thinking about mechanics—your weight, where your hands ought to be—and you forget the basic thing, about trying to be offensive in your mind and tagging the ball. That happened to me tonight.

Dave McNally was pitching for the Orioles, and I usually hit him pretty good. But the first time up, I took three straight pitches—three straight strikes. I was thinking about mechanics. I was thinking so hard I forgot to swing.

The Orioles beat us again. They knocked us back down to .500. They had us, 3-0, and our Tiger Finish fell one run short, 3-2. I'm depressed now, and our whole club is down.

Personally, I'm all confused. I don't know what to do. Tonight I thought drinking might work. It didn't. The bars closed too quick on me, before I could get myself real high. I tried sneaking into the house, and my wife caught me. She started giving me a lecture on leading that kind of life, and I just wasn't up to it. What I'd like to do right now is get in my car, all by myself, and go out in the middle of some lake and just fish and drink beer all day long.

May 1

This game is beautiful. I don't think there's anything in the world that can produce so many emotional highs and lows day in and day out. Yesterday, I was as downhearted as a man can be. Today, I . . . am . . . a . . . hero.

I hit a two-run homer off Jim Palmer, Denny pitched a shutout, and we beat the Orioles, 2-0.

In batting practice, I'd been working at standing away from the plate a little bit, but I must've forgotten to try it in a game. The first time I was up today, one of Palmer's pitches hit me in the left arm. When he came to bat, he said, "Hey, that pitch I hit you with was almost a strike."

I started thinking—"I must be crowding the plate"—and the next time up, I moved off maybe two inches. I hit Palmer's first pitch out of the park. I'm going to have to buy him a drink and thank him for the batting tip.

Before the game, Hank Aguirre, who'd pitched for us

all through his career until last year, dropped by to say hello. He's with the Chicago Cubs now. When he was with us, he always seemed to run into bad luck. One day, when a couple of bad hops cost him a game, he walked back to the dugout, looked to the heavens, raised his hands, and said, "Lord, Lord, get that black cloud away. It's been following me all my life. It's not bad enough to be a Mexican-American by descent and have to live with that, but all these bad hops and little clunkers that these guys are hitting, Lord, that is too much."

We always used to kid Hank, "Don't come near me, get out of here, get that black cloud away from me." And last year, the first year he wasn't with us since 1958, we won the pennant and told him the reason was that he'd taken his black cloud with him. He said today that maybe he had forgotten to take the cloud to Chicago. The Cubs are running away with their division. They're the Baltimore Orioles of the National League.

May 2

We're on the road again, and the Red Sox beat us, 3-2. I had another two-run home run. That's two nights in a row I've been the total offense for our club. I'm not enough. I don't know what's wrong with us. What surprises me is that Mayo still hasn't had a meeting to chew anybody's tail end off. There are other things than just hitting that are wrong with our club right now. We're not mentally sharp, we're not hustling like we can. Mayo, I don't know what you can say, but say something. Yell at us.

May 3

We lost again—now we're under .500—and I'd sure like to know what's going through Mayo's mind. I asked Wally Moses, Mayo's closest friend, why we haven't had any meetings, and Wally said, "Well, what can the man say that you guys don't know?"

Maybe Wally's right, and maybe he's right, too, when he keeps saying we're going to hit. But we'd better start soon or we'll all be able to get in some early October pheasant hunting.

May 4

We've got an exhibition game in Philadelphia tomorrow and my roommate, Joe Sparma, is going to pitch. He hasn't worked in a long time, and all he talks about is being traded. He figures the manager's completely given up on him.

We're all down. We lost to the Red Sox again today and slipped two games under .500, seven games behind Baltimore. They're twelve games over .500—just where I'd hoped we'd be by late July.

After the game, I stopped in at a local bar, a lively place that the football player, Gino Cappelletti, owns a piece of. Before long, there were so many Tigers in the place that someone said they'd be taking the team picture at ten.

May 5

Instead of having a day off, we played in Philadelphia today. The game was for charity, and we gave at the ball park. They beat us, 3-0, and about the only fun for me was the chance to see Richie Allen of the Phillies on his home turf. He arrived just before game time, wearing a big fur coat and stepping out of his big chauffeured Cadillac. He threw on a uniform, walked to the plate in a, shall we say, dazed condition, got a couple of hits and left before the fifth inning. He's beautiful.

Later, when we were riding the bus to the airport, the black slum area of Philadelphia greeted us with rocks.

One rock broke a window, another thudded against the side of the bus, and someone shouted, "Turn off the lights."

Earl Wilson had more sense. "Leave the lights on," he said, "and put us soul brothers at the windows."

Jim Northrup, who once played winter ball in Latin America, said that after close games there, he and the other players would climb into the bus, flop down on the floor, and let the debris fly by. Northrup also talked about the piece of concrete that someone threw out of the center-field bleachers in Boston a few days ago and caught him in the back. He still has a large welt. Then there were the fans in New York, who threw fruit and cherry bombs on the field the last time we played there. "They've got as much respect for you as an alligator has for a deer in the middle of a swamp," Northrup said.

The fans in Detroit don't always behave too sweetly, either. I wonder what they'll throw at us to greet us tomorrow night. The ways things are going, I may join them.

May 6

In the ninth inning tonight, with Denny McLain pitching, we were four runs up on the Kansas City Royals. And we lost. To an expansion team. I've never seen the locker room so dark and quiet.

I cannot believe Denny. When we got in from Philadelphia last night, his little Cessna airplane was warming up the minute our United charter touched ground. He bounced off one plane and into the other and was off to play the organ at a nightclub in Windsor, Ontario. The night before he was pitching. Denny says he's an organist first and a baseball player second, but without baseball he would be—well, how many organists can you name?

He shouldn't have been beaten by Kansas City tonight. He got a little tired, but, going into the ninth, leading 6-2, he was laughing and joking—and getting careless. When he got into trouble early in the inning, Mayo walked to the mound, and Denny convinced the manager not to take him out. He didn't leave until the score was 6-4.

Radatz came in, with two men on base and two out. All he had to do was to get one out and the game would be over. "Who's up, Mayo?" Radatz said.

"Hawk Taylor," Mayo said.

"Who's he?" one of the guys at the mound said.

"Who's he?" said Radatz. "I'll tell you who he is. He's as good as out."

We'd had a meeting before the game, the first since opening day, and after Mayo'd finally chewed on us a little for playing like individuals—for not hitting behind the runners and playing like a team as we did last year—the pitchers and catchers had gone over the Kansas City lineup man by man. According to our scouting report, Hawk Taylor was a high-fast-ball hitter. So, Radatz threw him a low fast ball, and Taylor hit it into the upper deck to beat us.

I wasn't much help myself. Each year I play a few games at first base, but every spring training, when I ask Mayo if he wants me to work out at that position, he says, "No, no, don't worry. You're not going to play first base this year. Don't even get a glove."

So, tonight, as I came into the locker room, Mayo peeked around the corner and said, "Come here, I want to talk to you."

I knew by the look in his eye what he was going to say. "You know," he said, "Norm hasn't been doing too good against left-handers and they got a left-handed kid named Butler pitching against us. Can you play first base?"

What could I say? "Well, sure," I said. "I'll try and do my best."

I did try, too, but I let in a run. I thought the umpire called one of their runners out at third, but he hadn't; he'd just made sort of a guttural sound. So when the runner rounded third, then stopped, I thought that was the third out and I stood there and ate the ball while he scored. Then we lost by one run.

When I got home, my wife, who'd turned off the radio in the seventh inning, said, "What score did we win by?"

"We lost, 7-6," I said.

"You're putting me on," she said.

For ten minutes, she thought I was kidding.

"Look, if you don't believe me," I said finally, "call the newspaper." Hell, I didn't want to believe it myself.

May 7

Driving home from the game tonight, I was listening to some music and, after playing a record the disk jockey said, "Hey, guess what, folks? A miracle happened. The Tigers finally won."

May 8

At 1:15 A.M., one hour and fifteen minutes into my first day off in three weeks, a day I'd set aside for sailing with my family, the rain started. The way things have been going, I really expected locusts.

May 9

The temperature was about thirty-nine tonight, rain had fallen on and off for twenty hours, the outfielders were standing in an inch of water, and we played. The decision to start the game was our management's. The owner, the general manager, and the other executives sit in an enclosed booth up behind first base. The weather was fine there.

Obviously, their decision was based on finances. We had a good advance sale, and if we postponed the game, we'd have to play a doubleheader Sunday, the day after tomorrow. But we don't need any bonus attraction Sunday, because it's Cap Day and we already have a big crowd coming. So we played tonight.

Dean Chance pitched for the Minnesota Twins. He hits me with pitches three or four times a year; naturally, I have a tendency to be a little intimidated by his sweeping right-handed motion. Instead of striding straight into the ball, I sometimes step towards third base, moving away from that inside pitch. This is fine for safety, but bad for batting, so after Chance struck me out my first time up, I went to our trainer and said to him, "Hey, you got any nails in your medicine kit?"

"Nails?" he said. "What for?"

"Want to tack my left foot down so it won't fly toward third base."

Chance beat us, and if that weren't enough, someone called the ball park and said he was going to kill Al Kaline during the game. The management called the police and told them, then called the Secret Service and told them. But nobody told Al until after the game. They were afraid, I guess, that Al might decide not to play and that would hurt our offense. Our offense? What about the man's life?

May 10

A year ago today, Denny McLain beat the Washington Senators, and we moved into first place and stayed there every day the rest of the season.

Today, we were rained out. By our current standards, that's success.

My throwing arm is killing me, especially the tendon just above the elbow, so, with a day off, I went down to the hospital for X rays. There aren't any bone chips or serious problems—just a strain, an irritation of the tendons. I did it by throwing. A catcher throws more than anybody else. Although a pitcher throws with greater velocity, a catcher throws day after day after day, and elbow trouble—from the strain—is nothing new for me. Some years I've had as many as six to ten cortisone shots.

Last year I had a bad arm at the beginning of the season, too, and the runners in the league took advantage of it. This year they've been having some success with me, too. One of these days, I'll catch up to them. I hope.

May 11

I played first base again, and the way Jim Price has been catching and hitting, I don't know when I'll get back behind the plate. The pitchers say they like throwing to Jimmy. When I read that in the papers, well, I figure I'm the first-string catcher and I just want to get out there and do a little bit better. Jimmy and I have a lot of respect for each other, and I'm always pulling for him. But I still want my job back.

As for first base, I usually kid Norm Cash by telling him it's like a day off for me when I'm out there. But not today. The sun was dodging in and out, and I don't really know how to use sunglasses and I misjudged two pop-ups. I also had trouble with grounders. I tell myself to just get in front of them and knock them down. A couple of times today, I banged the ball down with my chest, found it lying in front of me, and had time to pick it up and get the runner at first. Late in the game, when we were protecting a one-run lead, I prayed as hard as I could that they wouldn't hit any shots at me. McLain survived me, though, and beat the Twins, 3-2.

Afterward I went to see Mayo. He'd posted a sign on the bulletin board saying we would have a workout tomorrow, and for three months my family and I have been planning to spend the day up north, in the vacation house we own on a lake in Lewiston, Michigan. I just had to lie to the man. I told him my family was already up at the house and the only way they could get back was if I picked them up. He wasn't happy, but he told me I could go.

We left for the lake as soon as I got home. I hooked the boat to the car, started to back out of the garage, caught the garage door, and ripped the top off the boat. I'll never lie to Mayo again.

May 12

Up here, in the woods, I can relax. I took the kids out fishing during the day, and at night my wife and I built a fire, turned on some records, and just looked out at the moon over the lake. I can't think of any place in the world I'd rather be.

May 13

We drove down from the lake today, back to reality in three hours of superhighway. I went out to the park early and worked on bat speed, one of the keys to good hitting.

Then it rained. We started the game half an hour late, then had to stop for an hour when the rain came again in the seventh inning. We were at bat when the game was delayed; Willie Horton was up with two strikes on him, and Norm Cash was on first base. During the delay, Cash said he'd run out to second base when we resumed. He did it.

"What are you doing down here?" the umpire at second base said.

"I stole second during the rain," Cash said. "Didn't you see me?"

Lolich, who was pitching for us, decided he wasn't going to warm up after the hour's delay. It puts a lot of strain on the arm to just go out and start pitching without warming up, but Mick doesn't take very good care of his arm. He's a big guy with a super arm, and even when he starts spring training, he throws as hard as he does all year. After the rain tonight, our pitching coach, John Sain, was just shaking his head. "One of these days," John said, "he's going to wake up and not have that great arm and he won't know how to take care of himself."

But not last night. Mick beat the White Sox, 3-1. We're one game under .500 now, and of our fourteen victories, McLain and Lolich have won nine. We're starting to hit better. Maybe we've turned ourselves around.

May 14

Gary Peters shut us out tonight, but, really, we're starting to hit again. We're attacking the ball, hitting line drives. We hit them right at people tonight, but they'll start to fall in.

Willie Horton probably hit the ball best. But he got robbed on a couple of spectacular catches, and when he had some trouble in the field, the fans booed him. They wouldn't let up, and Willie's sensitive about things like that. Fans are so fickle. Forty thousand of them showed up at the airport last October to greet us after we'd won the World Series, and I'll bet that some of the same 40,000 were booing tonight. They're front-runners, and our biggest fault now is that we won the pennant last year. Luis Aparicio of the White Sox, who's played on winners and losers, came up to bat tonight, turned to me, and said, "If you don't win this year, you're going to be booed all over the place."

Before the game tonight, I was given a Gold Glove award as the best defensive catcher in the American League last year. The selection's made by the coaches and managers in the league, and it's quite an honor. Mickey Stanley got a Gold Glove award, too, as the best center fielder. But Mickey's playing shortstop now, and he's had trouble adjusting. So much of success in this game comes from mental attitude—having confidence, being able to relax, and let your reflexes and responses move you along naturally. Mickey hasn't been able to do that. He's thinking too much; he's so concerned with mechanics, he's a half-beat behind in his reactions. There's no time to think about the right way to make a play and *then* make the play. You just have to do it.

I caught the game, and I'm no Gold Glove catcher right now. My arm's killing me. I thought the rest I had playing first base would help, but the arm's about to fall off. The doctors still say there's nothing wrong but tendon irritation. I don't know. I think I'll get a cortisone shot tomorrow. If they stick that cortisone into exactly the right spot, it can give you 100 percent movement immediately.

If I do get a shot, it'll be in a closed training room. Only my trainer will know. I never tell people when there's anything wrong with my arm. If I did, it would get in the papers and the opponents would start running on me. Last year, when the papers reported I had arm trouble, I lied and denied it. I don't even tell my teammates; sometimes there's a lot of barroom talk with players on other teams, and that's the same as putting it out on the television networks.

We go on the road again in two days, but we got some good news today. Instead of staying over in Minnesota on our off-day, next Monday, we're coming home for a day, then going to Chicago. My wife says she's going to take back all those mean, nasty things she's said about our traveling secretary. He's not really a mean old man who takes fiendish delight in taking her husband away. She loves him—this week.

May 15

Tommie John pitched against us for the White Sox tonight. A year ago, he hit Dick McAuliffe with a pitch, and they had a fight out at the mound. John got a broken collarbone, and was out for the season; McAuliffe was suspended for five days. Today was the first time they'd faced each other since the battle, and you could sense the excitement in the crowd. Nothing happened. Dick walked, and that was it.

In the tenth inning, Dick got a base hit and won the game for us, 2-1. By then, John was out of the game and so was our starting pitcher, Earl Wilson. Earl pitched a tremendous game, and it was rough on him not getting the win. We just haven't scored any runs for him all year. He doesn't have a win yet even though he's been pitching well. After the game, Cash ran up to him in the locker room and said, "Hey, Earl, hang in there. You can't win them all."

Earl was soaking his elbow in ice, and he looked up at Pat Dobson, who'd pitched the tenth inning and got the win. Then he laughed. "You're all a bunch of prejudiced bastards," he said. "You wait until the white pitcher comes along until you score."

The fans were on Willie Horton again, and the third time he was up, I was in the on-deck circle and saw him looking up at the stands, trying to pick out the guys who were booing. I could see it was really getting to him, gnawing at him.

Willie'd popped up his first time and struck out his second time and now he struck out again. He walked right off the field and into the locker room, took off his uniform, showered, and left the park—in the middle of the game. Cash, Stanley, Gates Brown, and Ron Woods tried to talk him out of it, but Willie wouldn't listen. He's all mixed up right now. I wish the fans would realize the more pressure on a guy, the worse he's going to perform. He's struggling, he's trying, and they boo him. They can be so cruel— and then ask for your autograph afterward.

Right after the game, Mayo locked the clubhouse and had a meeting. "I'm sure that some of you guys, especially you guys in the bullpen, don't know that Willie took a shower and left after we asked him to stay," the manager said. "The press will be coming in here and asking you questions about it. I just want you to know what happened. There will probably be a fine and something said about it, but try not to make too big a thing with the press, because Willie's just confused right now and he's going to straighten out."

Mayo didn't look too happy. "I know the breaks have been going against us," he said, "but if we keep trying, they're going to go our way. And we're going to win this thing yet."

Horton was only missing at the end. Denny McLain was missing from the beginning. He called up the trainer and said he had the flu. I'm not sure what variety he had because, while we were standing for "The Star-Spangled Banner," his plane flew overhead. At least, it sure looked like his plane.

The rules for Denny just don't seem to be the same as for the rest of us. Most of us have to be at the park at least two and a half hours before game time. Denny sometimes shows up five or ten minutes before a game. People used to say, before night games, that the best thing about baseball was that you couldn't beat the hours. In Denny's case, anyway, that's still true.

May 16

On the way to the airport today, I bet Jim Northrup a dollar Willie Horton would be on the plane. Northrup gave me 5-1 odds, and he won. No Willie. Well, we didn't miss him tonight in Minnesota; the game was rained out.

While we waited for the game to be called, I sat on the bench and talked with Mayo Smith. Mayo told me that after the clubhouse meeting yesterday, Jim Campbell, our general manager, wanted to go find Willie. "I told him not to," Mayo said. "Willie's got to call us. We're not going to call him. I don't want him back here if he's going to pout and mope, if we have to baby him. He's got to straighten himself out. When he calls us, then we'll know he wants to play."

Mayo and I chatted for a while, and I was fascinated, partly because I might want to manage someday and I can learn from him and partly because we haven't had many serious conversations. He told me that, by playing high-school football, he'd learned that baseball is much tougher on the psyche; football players can release their frustrations by hitting somebody, he said, but in baseball, the pressures just build and build. He told me he hadn't understood much about the mental part of baseball until the year he managed a guy who had a deep psychological problem—exhibitionism. The man straightened out after psychiatric help, and Mayo himself started talking to psychiatrists and psychologists and reading books about psychology, learning to understand the way different pressures affect different people.

I've played for a lot of managers now, and Mayo, I guess, is the smartest at understanding personalities. He treats us as individuals. He treats us like men, not children. I only wish we could all live up to that.

Denny McLain was supposed to pitch tonight, but because of the rain, he'll work tomorrow—a Saturday national television game—and Mickey Lolich, who was scheduled to go tomorrow, will pitch Sunday. Mickey wasn't happy. "Things are really going against me," he said. "I had a chance to do what Denny usually does—pitch on national TV and get all that exposure—and the rain gives the chance right back to him."

May 17

We were shooting to get up to .500 today, playing the tough Minnesota Twins, and, once we got a 5-0 early lead, Denny McLain and Norm Cash started thinking more about the post-game network TV show than about the game. NBC gives $100 to the postgame guest—the star of the day—and by the seventh inning, Norm, who had a home run, another hit, and two runs batted in, announced that he was the front-runner for the $100.

McLain took offense. "Hey," he said, "I got a shutout going." They started a little competition and it built up in the eighth and ninth innings. Cash came to bat in the ninth, feeling that one more hit would get him on the show. He topped the first pitch down the first base line, waved his arms, trying to wish the ball foul. It rolled foul. Then Norman hit a pop-up, and he blew that ball foul and out of play. We were cracking up on the bench.

Norm got the count to 3-2, then foul-tipped the next pitch. John Roseboro, the Minnesota catcher, had the ball in his mitt, then fumbled it to the ground. McLain was sitting on the bench and rooting against Cash. He hollered at Roseboro, "C'mon, catch the ball." Then McLain yelled to Bob Miller, who was pitching for the Twins, "Throw him a breaking ball. He won't hit it."

Cash turned to Roseboro and said, "Hey, this is a $100 pitch. I got to hit it."

Roseboro called for a curve, and Norm popped out to center field. Roseboro looked at our dugout and gave McLain the high sign, sort of saying. "There, I took care of him."

Mayo, understandably, was getting a little concerned. We still had three outs to go. Mayo sat there, gritting his teeth and wondering. I was, too. I could see that if McLain started screwing around, I'd have to get on his tail real quick. I knew that his arm had been bothering him the whole game, that he wasn't pitching too well, that although he'd been getting guys out, he hadn't been overpowering them. But he went out there, this man who makes at least $150,000 a year from baseball and other interests, and, sniffing that $100, reached back and threw the blazes out of the ball. He struck out Harmon Killebrew on four pitches. Cash was down at first base, rooting for Harmon, yelling, "Hit a home run." If the Twins broke up the shutout, Cash figured, he'd still have a chance to be on the show.

McLain got the Twins out, one-two-three, went on the show, then came into the locker room with the $100 bill pasted to his forehead. It was the best inning he'd pitched. He had to show us that when he wants to do it, he can.

I walked into the locker room, and Mayo said, "That man will never cease to amaze me."

"I feel the same way," I said.

"You know," Mayo said, "I was nervous about that guy the whole game. I was tight all the time."

"I know," I said. "But the man sure pitched a ninth inning. The best thing you can do is offer him a hundred bucks every time he pitches a shutout."

May 18

Willie Horton is still among the missing. I can understand the pressures on him. We've all gone through it. Not exactly the same pressures—he's black and he's a hometown man, brought up in Detroit—but similar frustrations, similar problems. I don't hold anything against him. I just hope he comes back soon.

Mickey Lolich was a little concerned before the game today. "Looks like the guys did some celebrating last night," he said to me on the bus to the park. A few of the guys did look a little weary.

"Don't worry," I said. "They'll just pop a few greenies and get ready to go."

We were a little sluggish at the start of the game, but we got a 2-0 lead anyway. Then Billy Martin, the Minnesota manager, woke us up. He had two guys steal home —first Cesar Tovar, then Rod Carew—the first and second times in my career anyone had stolen home on me.

Both times Lolich took a big windup, and after the

game, when a couple of reporters asked me, "How come you didn't get those guys?" I said, "Well, sir, there is not a helluva lot I can do without the ball."

But, anyway, that woke us up. The next time Tovar came up, Lolich threw the ball high and tight and hit him right in the head. Martin began yelling from the bench. The next inning, his pitcher, Dave Boswell, threw at Al Kaline's head. Immediately, the first-base umpire, Ed Runge, the senior man in the umpiring crew, called time out and warned both managers that the next time a pitcher hit anybody or knocked anybody down, he'd be suspended from the game and fined. I thought Runge made a good decision. Both pitchers said later. "The ball slipped." What a coincidence.

Usually, the home-plate umpire would give the warning, but Runge did it because there was a young guy behind the plate, and he was struggling all day with ball-and-strike calls. Martin was all over him, yelling, complaining, and though I don't like to ride an umpire, especially a young guy, I yelled just to offset Martin. When I started griping, Martin hollered, "Hey, don't listen to Freehan 'cause he went to college and he's a major in psychology and he's going to talk you out of all this stuff." I just smiled—at Martin.

We won, 8-2. Finally, we're over .500—by a game.

May 19

This morning, on our off-day in Detroit, I woke up with a bad heel. I must have hurt it when I fell down running the bases yesterday. It felt pretty bad, but I couldn't tell my wife because she'd have made me stay home, and I had a golf date with Jim Northrup, Dick McAuliffe, and Don Wert. We're not supposed to play golf during the season, but none of us knows how to play the organ.

We played in the rain, me and Wert against Jim and

Dick. Dick missed three putts of less than three feet, and each time "Sweet Lips" called him a choke-up artist. The best player on our team was Northrup the way he was agitating his partner.

Later, I went over to my dad's office and we went out and looked at some land for a commercial campground we want to develop. We need about fifteen to thirty acres, and none of the plots we saw seemed right.

I got home kind of late, and my wife was a little upset. She's usually upset when I'm out on business deals, because she wants to know about all my financial setups and investments, and I'm not too big on telling her. I don't think she knows that much about it, and as long as she's eating and buying clothes, that's all she's got to worry about. We got in a little argument about that, which is par for the course, but I won. She's a great wife, but I'm just not going to let her get involved in finances. She's too conservative; she thinks the best investment is a large savings account in the bank.

After dinner, watching television, we heard that Willie Horton was coming back to the club. The night before, one of the local television reporters had quoted Willie as saying he didn't want to play for Detroit any more. Well, I knew Willie didn't say that, and here was the proof, but this guy came on the air again today and insisted that what he'd said about Willie wanting to be traded was true. He knew it was true, he said, because, "Willie didn't call me up and tell me it wasn't true and he was home all day, heard all three of my broadcasts, and if anything was in there that wasn't true, I'm sure he would have called me."

The man's reasoning made no sense. Why would Willie even think of giving that man the satisfaction of calling him up to deny things that he dreamed up? Some of the people in the news media are only concerned about attention for themselves. They just don't pay any attention to their subject's feelings. As far as I'm concerned, you can take those guys who want sensationalism at an athlete's expense and throw them as far as you want.

May 20

We flew to Chicago today, and before we left, reporters and photographers and TV people were all over Willie Horton. "Hey, get up and just leave the man alone," Earl Wilson yelled at the newsmen. "Let the man up."

I wanted to go up to Willie and try to cheer him up a little, but I didn't know exactly what to say. So, I just walked up to him before the game and said, "Hey, it's nice to have you back. Don't worry about what's behind. Just worry about what's in front of you."

Mayo watched Willie hit in batting practice, then put him in the lineup. His first time up he hit a bases-loaded double. Willie ended up with two hits and three RBIs, and we beat the White Sox.

After the game, Willie dressed quickly and didn't say too much. His bat did the talking for him.

They've spruced up ancient Comiskey Park—or White Sox Park, as they call it now—with AstroTurf. When Dick Radatz saw the artificial grass, he began laughing. "This old beat-up park with new AstroTurf," he said. "That's like putting earrings on a pig."

May 21

We held our annual rookie boatride in Chicago today. We invited the rookies last night to a team boatride on the Chicago River and told them to be at the dock at eleven o'clock this morning. Naturally, they were going to be all alone. No veterans would be there. As a matter of fact, no boat would be there.

We've got four rookies this year—Dave Campbell, Mike

Kilkenny, Fred Scherman, and Ron Woods—and we figured the most likely to show up were Kilkenny and Scherman; they're young and haven't been around much. Campbell is twenty-seven and a graduate of the University of Michigan, and I figured that, just on the basis of his education, he'd be the least likely to fall for it.

But Dave always likes to be with the in-group, and he was real anxious to get on the boat. At ten this morning, he began calling up guys to make sure they were going. He called up Pat Dobson, and Dobson sort of yawned into the phone and said that he was a little tired after pitching the night before and didn't think he could make it. Then Dave called up Jim Price. Price disguised his voice and said, "Sorry, this is the valet. Mr. Price just left. Said he was going on a . . . does 'boatride' sound right?"

Campbell hustled down to the dock. When nobody else showed up, he had a big argument with a lady who was taking tickets for sightseeing tours on the Chicago River. She kept saying there's no such thing as a Tiger charter, and Dave kept saying there was. After a while, he knew he'd been put on—we Michigan grads are quick—so he came back to the hotel and began pounding on doors.

Nobody would let him in. Finally, Dave went to Dobson's room, knocked on the door and yelled, "Telegram." Dobson let him in, and Dave refused to leave and let Pat go back to sleep. We've been calling Campbell "C. A. Ballgame," because he always has a bat or a glove with him, but from now on we'll call him "C. A. Boatride."

There was a lot of laughing and joking before the game tonight. Some of us were talking about the new John Hancock Building, the tallest building in Chicago. The top of the building actually disappeared in the clouds today, and somebody said that our old luckless teammate, Hank Aguirre, must have taken an apartment there. When Hank goes out of town with the Cubs, the guy said, he just leaves his cloud on top of the building.

We never did get to play tonight. Rain and snow caused our third postponement in ten days. We can't complain. The way our pitchers have been performing, we have only two reliable starters—McLain and Lolich. Wilson's the third man, but he's been having bad luck, and nobody's filled that fourth spot. My roomie, Joe Sparma, has had a shot, and so have John Hiller and Pat Dobson, moving in from the bullpen. But nothing's worked. Pretty soon we're going to need a fourth pitcher.

May 22

We played the White Sox in Milwaukee tonight, and on the bus to the park, Grover Resinger, who was a coach with Chicago last year, started talking about Eddie Stanky. Eddie was the Chicago manager then, and he has, Grover said, one of the sharpest baseball minds ever, always two or three innings ahead of the other manager.

But I've heard a lot of people say that Stanky's one problem was handling men, that you couldn't play relaxed for him because he made you afraid to make a mistake. Once, I heard, when the players were particularly tight, Grover went to talk to Stanky in the manager's private office. "Eddie, I think some of the boys are a little tight," Grover said.

Stanky stared at him.

"You know," Grover said, "the guys aren't relaxed."

Still, Stanky stared.

"They're afraid to make mistakes," Grover said.

"What did you do?" Stanky said. "Read a book on psychology?"

"No," Grover said.

"Then get the hell out of here," Stanky said.

Don Gutteridge is the White Sox manager now. A couple of years ago, when Gutteridge was coaching for Stanky, I was blocking home plate in the bottom of the ninth—two out, Tommie Agee tagging up from third with the winning run, the throw flying in. The ball and Agee hit me at the same time, we went down hard into the dirt and, in the tangle, Agee was safe. Tony Cuccinello, the Chicago third-base coach, came running over to help up Agee. Gutteridge, coming in from first base, passed me and helped me up. Suddenly, Stanky stormed out of the dugout, screaming at Gutteridge for helping me. This was at the end of the season, and the next year Stanky didn't rehire Gutteridge.

Joe Sparma was really down before the game. My roomie hadn't pitched in two weeks, hadn't been asked to warm up in two weeks. We were in the training room, and Joe said, "I wonder if he even wants me on the field."

Just then, Mayo walked in. "Everybody on the field at 7:15 for player introductions," he said.

"Hey, Joe," I said. "What did you just say, Joe?"

"Hey, Skip," Joe said. "You want me out there?"

Silence.

"Me, Skip?" Joe said. "Remember me?"

"Yeah," Mayo said. "I said everybody. You're still part of this team, aren't you, Joe?"

Nobody laughed.

When Mayo walked out, I told Joe, "Hey, if it'll make you feel a little better, one of these days when we're going good and know we aren't going to have a close game or anything like that, I'll give you a call and tell you to warm up. Just for excitement's sake. Just to make you feel good. Just so you can hear your name on the bullpen phone."

"The only chance I've got of playing a game," Joe said, "is if the starter gets hurt warming up."

The starter, McLain, didn't get hurt tonight; he just got knocked out, and we lost, 7-3. We used a few relief pitchers, and Joe was one of them. He worked one inning and got three men out, and when Aparicio batted against him, Luis said to me: "What's the matter with this guy? Why isn't he pitching?"

"Right now, he's in the doghouse with the manager,"

I said, "and with the weather and everything, we haven't needed four pitchers."

"He's got a good arm," Aparicio said. Luis's right. Joe's got a great arm and some of the best natural talent I've ever caught. He's just having trouble putting it together, and the lack of work doesn't help.

McLain didn't take the loss too severely. In fact, by the time the game was over and we came into the locker room, Denny was gone. He'd packed his bags and his locker was empty, and he was on his way back to Chicago. I don't know how the manager feels, but some of the players are beginning to talk. Lolich, for one, says he wants to be allowed some of the same liberties.

Mickey did some nightclub singing last winter, and maybe he can get bookings now on the days he's not pitching.

May 23

For four innings against the California Angels tonight, Mickey Lolich was struggling. He had good speed, but he could hardly find the strike zone. When he started to warm up for the fifth inning, holding a 4-3 lead, he threw four straight pitches into the dirt. I didn't even wait for a batter to come up. I ran out to the mound.

Mickey and I have had some curious conversations at the mound during games. In the sixth inning of the seventh game of the 1968 World Series, the most important game of the year, the score was 0-0, and Lou Brock, the most dangerous runner on the Cardinals, was on first base with none out. The pressure was intense. I went out to the mound. "You all right?" I asked Mickey. "Anything I can do for you?"

"Yeah," he said. "Can you get me a couple of hamburgers between innings?"

We didn't get around to food in our conversation tonight. "What's the matter?" I said.

"Can't get myself together," Mickey said. "I don't know what I'm doing wrong."

"Want me to make a suggestion?" I said.

John Sain, our pitching coach, doesn't like a catcher to go out and offer suggestions to the pitcher. John feels it may disrupt the pitcher's concentration. But John says it's all right if the pitcher asks for a suggestion, so I asked Mickey to ask me.

Mick wanted to hear what I had to say, and I told him I thought he was rearing back too far, trying to throw the ball too hard every pitch. I told him to keep his front shoulder in, instead of rearing back. "Just try to throw strikes," I said, "and you'll still get good velocity from there."

After that, Mick was incredible. He struck out sixteen batters, a Detroit record. Strangely, neither Mickey nor I knew he was breaking any record. When the game ended, the crowd gave him a standing ovation. We came off the field together, and he said, "What are they clapping for?"

"I don't know," I said.

Then someone told us Mickey'd broken Paul Foytack's record of fifteen strikeouts set back in 1956. I remember listening to that game on the radio while I was caddying; now Paul's our batting-practice pitcher. "Nobody's going to remember you by tomorrow," one of the guys told Foytack, "because your name has just been *erased* from the record book."

In the clubhouse, Mick came over and thanked me for the tip. "I guess you knew what you were talking about," he said.

I'm glad I accomplished something tonight, because I sure didn't do much with the bat. My average was up to .280 for a while, but now it's slipped to about .270.

May 24

I'm dragging, mentally and physically, and the bone bruise on my heel is still hurting. In batting practice today, I was swinging way behind the ball, and Wally Moses was giving me the eagle eye. "Hey, Wally," I yelled. "It's Saturday morning. You know what Saturday morning is like."

Wally knew it wasn't just that. "You're tired," he said. "You ought to tell the manager you're tired. We're not machines. You ought to take yourself out." I couldn't. I've never yet asked a manager to rest me.

Kaline was probably even more tired than I. My wife was talking to Al's wife, Louise, and she said their two young boys got up this morning, made breakfast, and suddenly realized that Al and Louise had overslept. Al got to the park in the middle of batting practice. He looked like he was still asleep. Then he hit two home runs and won the game for us, bringing us three games over .500.

Earl Wilson got his second win this week, and I think he's all right again. Earl's had a lot of injuries the past year and a half, but he's strong now. I think he can win sixteen or seventeen games. He'd better if we're going to win the pennant. All we need is a fourth starting pitcher, and we'll be in pretty good shape.

The Angels have lost nine in a row now. Before the game, Mayo and I were talking to their manager, Bill Rigney. "I don't know what this meant," Rig said, "but Gene Autry (the Angels' owner) called me up last night and said, 'This isn't a vote of confidence, but you *are* going through hard times and things aren't going right for you, and we want you to know we are behind you 100 percent.'"

Mayo and Rig both laughed. They know what a vote of confidence means in baseball. You get that one day and you get fired two days later.

After the game, I went to a christening for my brother Bob's new son. It was nice to see my first nephew. Maybe one of these days I can have a boy. I'd like that. It's on my mind a lot now that my wife is pregnant.

We beat the Angels today, 10-0, and we had such a big lead so early that Kaline and I were taken out of the game. It was the first either of us had missed an inning all year, and I didn't mind coming out. My heel's hurting so much—when I'm hitting, it's difficult for me to put pressure on the front foot, to stride into a pitch firmly—that I had to get two cortisone shots during the game.

After the game, my wife mentioned to Al and Louise Kaline that she kind of felt sorry for the Angels; Mike Roarke, one of my early roommates in the big leagues, is their third-base coach. Louise Kaline looked at Pat and said that she didn't feel sorry for anybody else in this game. "If you don't take it from them," she said, "they're going to take it from you."

We're going good, finally. We've won nine games out of our last eleven, and we're four games over .500. The only difficulty is that when we started this streak, we were seven games behind Baltimore, and now we're eight games behind Baltimore. They've moved twenty games over .500—the season's only seven weeks old, and they've won about three-fourths of their games—and my roommate and I have developed a little routine.

"Guess what?" I say.

"What?" Joe says.

"The Orioles won today."

Sparma laughs. He doesn't get much amusement these days.

May 26

Mickey Lolich and I spent today on the West Coast, a day ahead of the rest of the team, so that we could make a dealer film for Dodge. The Tiger management was reluctant to let Mickey and me fly ahead. They insisted that our trip meant problems with the team travel insurance and with team discipline. I couldn't buy their arguments. I wanted to say, "You see, there's this pitcher. . . ." I didn't say that, but I won the argument, anyway.

May 27

Mickey and I started working on the Dodge film at eight o'clock last night in San Diego. We only had to get about six minutes of usable film. We finished after the sun came up this morning.

The film is one in a series to introduce the 1970 Dodge Polara models. It goes like this: Mickey and I walk out of a restaurant and look around. Some kids come up and ask for our autographs. Mickey signs first—with body paint on the back of some girl. Then a baker walks up with a cake, and I autograph the cake. That's it. And it took us ten hours. I think my future's in baseball.

Dodge has put together what they call an all-star sports staff—Fran Tarkenton, football; Lee Trevino, golf; Dave Bing, basketball; Mickey and myself, baseball. Last year Mickey won a Dodge Charger from *Sport* magazine for being the Most Valuable Player in the World Series, and then Mickey's agent got him a three-year promotional contract with Dodge. I'd been with Chrysler since 1963 —driving one of their cars and doing some local promotion, nothing that made me any real money—but after the World Series the Chrysler people sent me over to the Dodge Division, and Dodge offered me a great contract plus two cars a year. I signed with them. I don't know how long it will last, but the people there have been super so far.

Mickey and I flew up to Oakland this morning, went to sleep at 9:15 A.M. and got up at 4:15, just in time to get the five o'clock bus to the ball park—and Mickey was our starting pitcher. Mickey said he was so tired from being up all night making the commercial that he was thinking about asking Mayo to have someone else pitch. I felt just the opposite. I believe that when you do something extracurricular, like a commercial, you're not allowed to feel bad. You've got to be ready to play.

Mickey didn't say anything, and he started. He was wild, and they scored two runs in the first inning. I wasn't much help. Oakland stole three bases on me.

After the first inning, Mayo came over to me and said, "What time did you guys get in here this morning?"

I was nonchalant. "Oh, we flew in good and early," I said.

A couple of minutes later, when the skipper wasn't looking, I went over to Mickey, who was talking to someone down at the end of the dugout. "Hey, did Skip want to know when we got in?" he said.

"Yeah," I said. "I just told him that we came up in the morning. I didn't tell him we were up all night."

We got a 3-2 lead, and Mickey began pitching real well. Then, in the sixth inning, with two out and a man on third, Danny Cater, probably one of the most underrated players in baseball, hit a line drive off Mickey's left elbow. The tying run scored—we lost, eventually—and Mickey had to leave the game. The loss of the game wasn't as important as the loss of Lolich; he may be out a couple of weeks with swollen muscles. His record is 6-1, and we can't afford to lose our most consistent pitcher.

Oh, yes. Something else happened today. Bill Rigney got fired.

May 28

Daryl Patterson, a relief pitcher who helped us tremendously last year, got out of military service three weeks ago, and now he's ready to go back on the active roster. To stay within the legal limit of twenty-five players, Mayo had to take someone else off the list tonight—sell the man or release him or send him to the minors.

I figured that since Daryl's a right-handed relief pitcher, Dick Radatz might be the one to go. A couple of other guys I talked to before the game suspected the same thing.

We beat Oakland by a run tonight, the third victory in a row for Earl Wilson, and in the locker room afterward, we were pretty happy. I was sitting with Cash and Kaline and Northrup, and we were agitating and kidding around. Mayo was going around congratulating everybody. Mayo talked to us, then went over to Fred Scherman, the rookie pitcher. "Hey, Fred," he said, "Come on into my office for a second."

With Lolich out and a series with Seattle, an expansion team, coming up this weekend, it figured that Mayo would be giving a start to Fred. He's a lefty, like Mickey, a solid kid who's got a chance to be a good major-league pitcher. I'd been annoyed that Mayo had pitched him only two or three times all season because Fred's got potential and, more important, you need twenty-five contributing guys in this game, twenty-five guys you can move in and out, twenty-five guys who get work and stay sharp. We won the pennant last year because our twenty-five guys were better than anybody else's. It's not eight guys and it's not three pitchers that win a pennant; it's twenty-five people. You can't keep a guy like Scherman inactive too long because you're going to call on him to win a game someday and he'll need some sharpened skills and some confidence.

I was glad Mayo was calling Scherman to his office; so were Cash and Kaline and Northrup. We began agitating. "Now, hey, Fred," Al said. "Don't get nervous. You're going to be the starting pitcher on Saturday, on color TV and the game of the week."

"Yeah," Northrup said, "go on in there and don't get nervous—even if Seattle is a small park."

We were shaving when someone came over and said Scherman wasn't going to pitch in Seattle. He was going to the minors to make room for Patterson.

"I feel terrible," Kaline said. "We were joking about being nervous and the man gets sent down. What do you do now? How do you explain what you were just saying?"

I went up to Fred after I got dressed, and he was a little teary-eyed. Again, I can't really understand what some of those guys go through because it hasn't happened to me.

I felt a little squeamish. Being sympathetic has never been one of my strong suits. You hate to go with the same cliche stuff: "Well, stay in there; if you pitch well, you'll be back here." You know, the same glad hand, pat-'em-on-the-back routine that most guys give.

I talked to Fred a little bit and tried to give him some encouragement. He was upset. "I've showed 'em for a couple of years now that I can pitch Triple-A," he said, "and they brought me up here and never gave me a chance. Well, why send me back to Triple-A? I know I can pitch there. I want to show 'em I can pitch *here*."

Fred had been with the club since the beginning of the season, and he and his wife had rented a house in Detroit for the summer. Fred didn't want to have to pay up the lease, so he just went up to Daryl Patterson and asked if he'd like to take over the house. Daryl felt pretty funny. First he comes up and takes Fred's job, then he takes Fred's house. Daryl said he felt like a vulture. But that's the life that goes with baseball. You know when you sign your contract that eventually it's going to happen. It's going to happen to me.

May 29

Mayo came up to me before the game in Oakland today and wanted to know how I was feeling. "Oh, not too bad," I said. I've been wearing a pad on my heel and it's a little uncomfortable. I can't run or turn the corner very good, but I can still play. And I want to.

"I was thinking of maybe catching Jimmy today," Mayo said.

"You're the boss," I said. "Do whatever you want." But I wanted to play.

"Well," Mayo said. "I'm going to give you the day off, and we'll let Jimmy play 'cause he's swinging the bat pretty good."

Until today, in the two and a half years he's been here, Mayo's only benched me when I've had a bad injury, or for the second game of a doubleheader. It was a record I was proud of.

I spent the day in the bullpen. I don't usually go down there because it drives me crazy. I don't know how anybody can sit in the bullpen and pay attention to a game; it's probably the worst seat in the park. But it was a nice sunny day and I went down there, and Al Kaline did, and Dave Campbell, too, and we were all sitting with our hats off, chewing sunflower seeds, and getting tanned. There were so many guys in the bullpen the manager had to call a few back to the bench.

Our bullpen guys are constantly agitating each other. They needle about some pitch a guy may have made a couple of nights before, or about some feature of a guy's anatomy. There's a constant state of agitation, much of it obscene. Don McMahon just sits in his own corner and tries to watch the game, but the other guys pretty much forget about the game. I don't see how they can do it because I live and die with what happens out on the field. When I'm out of a game, when I see things going wrong, I guess I feel like the fan who said last year that it's a lot easier to play those games in the pennant race than it is to watch them. If you're just sitting there watching, you're holding your breath too much.

You need a special kind of temperament to sit in the bullpen. Terry Fox, a relief pitcher with the Tigers when I broke in, had the best bullpen temperament I've ever seen. Terry's job was late-inning relief, and he'd go down to the bullpen, get off into a corner and go to sleep —not a deep sleep, but a semisleep. He'd wake up about the fifth inning, take a chew of tobacco, drink a little water, and start getting himself charged up. He'd get his glove on, watch the game a little, then, about the seventh inning, he'd be ready to jump right in and do his job.

We won today, even though for the second day in a row the stadium organist drove our pitcher crazy. Last night, the organist kept playing while Mickey Lolich was winding up, and in the second inning I simply told the umpire I wasn't going to call any signals until that guy stopped the music. Today, the guy did it to McLain. Denny balked at one point and blamed the organist. He really blasted the guy afterward. First of all, Denny said, the guy had no business playing when he was in his windup; second, Denny said, the guy couldn't play worth a damn, and third—and here's where Denny got angriest —the guy wasn't even playing a Hammond organ. Denny, understand, endorses the Hammond organ.

Norm Cash got a little upset, too. He sliced a ball on the ground to first base, thought it was foul, and didn't run very hard. The ump called it fair, and Norm was out. As he ran back to the dugout, Norm shouted at the umpire, "I hope you guys all go out on strike. We'll do better on the honor system."

May 30

We'd heard that the Seattle ball park was pretty small, and we weren't disappointed. At least, the hitters weren't.

It's a hitter's park, which makes it exciting for us and the fans. In a small park, no matter how many runs you get behind, there's always a chance to come back. Boston's park is like that, and Detroit's, and now Seattle's. No safe leads. Plenty of tension. I think it'd be better for baseball if the new parks are all small. Everybody likes to see hitting.

Almost everybody. After one look at the field, John Hiller, our starting pitcher, began walking around with a hat, collecting money from all the hitters. "I'm taking up a collection for the Shell-shocked Pitcher's Fund," he said.

In a park like this, you've got to fight a tendency to overswing; you've got to try to hit line drives. The home runs'll come. When the Orioles came in here, they lost their first game because they were trying to swing for the hills. We were smart today. Kaline went with pitches twice, slicing line drives to right field. Cash knocked in a run with a hit to the opposite field. Northrup gave a ball his "short stroke" and hit it out of this world, completely over the temporary bleachers.

Wayne Comer, who was with us last year and hit only one home run all season, is a slugger here. He's a big buddy of Willie Horton's and, once, when Wayne came up today, I said, "Willie said hit one to him." Wayne hit the next pitch about eighty feet over Willie's head. When Wayne got back to the plate after running out his home run, I said, "Hey, I'm not going to talk to you any more."

The Pilots hit more home runs than we did, but we won the game.

Later, in the locker room, Mayo reminded us that for tomorrow's game we have to leave for the park at 9:45 in the morning. Curfew's midnight, he said, and anyone who misses it will be fined a couple of hundred dollars. Someone said, "Aah, wait a minute, Mayo, we're winning."

And Mayo answered, "That'll be double for you."

I'm upset by the fact that I'm still not throwing well. I've had more third-base steals on me this year than ever before. The writers are on me constantly, trying to find out if my arm is all right. Well, I've got a couple of things wrong with my arm—the tendon's bothering me, and there's a place on the back of my arm that's bothering me—but I won't tell those people. They'll put it in the paper, and I'm trying to protect something.

I hate being away from home on a holiday. I know the weather's nice back in Detroit this Memorial Day weekend. I talked to my wife and she said the kids were out playing, and she was planting flowers and I thought of all the picnics people are on and I'm busting my tail trying to play a game 2,500 miles from home.

I was at dinner with Mickey Stanley and Jim Northrup, and Stanley said, "It'd be real nice if they could give you one week off during the summer just to spend with your family, to go on a picnic, or go to a lake."

"All you got to do," said Northrup, "is jump the club and not get paid for a week, and pay a thousand dollars fine besides."

Mickey said he couldn't afford that yet.

May 31

The other night, my roomie went to what we call a prayer meeting—other people call them poker games—and I guess his prayers for inside straights didn't come through. Before the game today, Sparma said he had only $6.50 in his pocket. But he was going to be the starting pitcher, and the game was on national TV, so he said he'd pick up some walking-around money, being the star of the game and getting $100 for the postgame show.

"Forget it," Cash said. "I'm going to win the hundred."

"No," Joe said. "This is a big weekend for Italians. Andretti and Granatelli won at Indianapolis yesterday, and now it's time another dago did something that'll make him famous."

Joe had pitched only five or six innings in three weeks. He needs to pitch a lot to have his control, so we were hoping that maybe we'd get four or five strong innings from him. The first inning was a tip-off to the kind of struggle it was going to be. He walked the first guy, Tommy Harper, on four pitches. Harper's leading both leagues in stolen bases, and I've been having all this trouble throwing guys out, so he took off for second right away. I threw him out.

Joe walked the next man, Mike Hegan, on four pitches, then the third batter, Tommy Davis, swung at a bad ball, and we got a double play. We got three guys out, and still Joe hadn't thrown one pitch over the plate.

Joe kept struggling. I was constantly getting on him, chewing him out, trying to get him mad so he'd keep his concentration. I'd throw the ball back at him hard. He was in trouble all the time, but he kept getting guys out. In the fifth inning, when Seattle got two men on base, Mayo came out to talk to Joe. I didn't think Mayo was going to bring in another pitcher. For all his troubles, Joe was pitching a no-hitter.

"Now, listen, just settle down," Mayo told him. "Relax a little bit. Don't try to muscle them. Just try to throw the ball for strikes."

Joe's no-hitter was still working after the eighth inning, and I was getting real excited. I've never caught a no-hitter in professional baseball. Joe knew what he had going; the scoreboard kept staring him in the face. I sat between Joe and John Sain during the top of the ninth, and I said to Joe, "You got anything on your mind?"

He said, "Yeah. Next inning, let's go to throwing breaking balls, a lot of curves."

"Okay," I said, "as long as you throw them for strikes." Then I looked at Sain and started laughing. "Joe's in trouble now," I said. "He's thinking."

Joe got the first hitter out in the ninth, then Don Mincher came up. Mincher's one of the toughest batters in the Seattle lineup. Joe had had trouble with him all game, and we would have liked to have walked him. But we couldn't. We were only ahead by two runs, and we couldn't purposely bring the tying run to the plate. So Joe pitched and Mincher hit a long shot to center field, and the ball fell in for a double. To help us defensively, Mayo had moved Mickey Stanley out to center field in place of Northrup. Mickey's probably the best center fielder in the game and there was no way he could have caught the ball, but after the inning, after Joe'd got two more outs and won with a one-hitter, I began to agitate Mickey. "See what happens," I said, "when Mayo goes and makes a move. Northrup probably would have caught the ball."

"Hey, don't say that," Mickey said, and he was glaring at me. "I should've gotten that ball and that's nothing to make fun of."

I bit my tongue; I didn't realize Mickey was so sensitive. Later, I apologized. "I didn't think you could have caught the ball, Mickey," I said. "I was just joking. Lord, the guy got a hit and that was the end of it." Mickey cooled off.

Of course, Joe got on the postgame show, came back with the $100, and started to agitate Cash about it. The guys call Joe "Square-Deal Ralph," because he's like that used-car dealer Johnny Carson's always talking about, Ralph Williams of Los Angeles. Joe always has some fast business deal going for him. Now, when Joe came back, Kaline, who'd brought in the ball after the last out, went up to him. "Ralph," Kaline said to Joe, "you want the game ball?"

"Sure," Joe said.

"Okay, here it is," Al said. "That'll be fifty dollars down and a dollar a day for the rest of your life."

Although it's against league rules, when a pitcher throws a no-hitter it's customary for his club to give him a $1,000 bonus. Jim Campbell, our general manager, rode back on the bus with us, and Joe began yelling, "I saved you a helluva lot of money, Campbell. How about splitting it with me?"

"There's nothing in your contract says I have to," Campbell said.

"Well, I need the money bad," Joe said, "so see if you couldn't at least advance me a hundred after all that money I saved you."

"Forget it," I told Campbell. "But how about the $200 I get for telling Mincher what pitch was coming just to save you a grand?"

June 1

After winning four in a row, we got beat by Seattle this afternoon, 8-7. Usually, if you go on a road trip and play three games in each town and win two out of three in each town, you're all right. You win pennants playing .667 baseball. But this year, the way the Orioles are playing, when we win two out of three, we either stand still or lose ground.

I almost passed out during the game—from something called fibrillations of the heart. I get them maybe three or four times a year. The muscle that regulates the heartbeat gets stimulated for some reason and all of a sudden the heart will race, then stop momentarily, then start racing again. Often, it just does that for a moment or two, then the beat becomes normal again. But when it goes on for a while—racing, stopping, racing—it takes all the wind out of you. It exhausts you. You can't take a deep breath.

I've had these fibrillations since grade school. Sometimes they're activated by a sharp movement; I remember they started once when I just popped up in class to answer a question. Sometimes they're activated by something as simple as rolling over in bed. They're not dangerous, the doctors tell me, and they don't mean any heart defect; they're simply a symptom of an overactive heart.

They rarely occur during a game. The club wasn't even aware that I had these things until my fifth season. I broke up a double play one day, hitting the shortstop as he threw to first, and the ball cracked into my helmet. The impact set off the fibrillations and when I told the manager, he took me out of the game. I was sent to the hospital and my heart kept racing and stopping all night. They had an electrocardiogram on me, and the thing went wild. I kept telling the doctor that they'd go away if he'd just let me get up and walk around or do something natural. They stop by themselves, usually, I told him, but the more I think about them, the longer they last.

Finally, about ten in the morning, I persuaded a nurse to let me out of bed. I took a shower—first hot, then cold, a lot of switching to start me thinking about anything but that pumping—and the fibrillations went away. I'd had an electrocardiogram reading right before the shower and it was completely irregular. Ten minutes later, after the shower, I had another one and it was completely normal.

The doctors have told me that if I don't smoke and don't drink much alcohol or coffee, it helps. Well, last night I had a few more drinks than I should have because Joe and I went out and celebrated his one-hitter. And today the fibrillations started up after I scored from second base on a double.

The trainer and I have a routine for them by now, so when I got to the dugout and told him, he began pinching my neck. That stops the blood going to the heart and sometimes immediately stops the fibrillations. It didn't work today. The heart kept racing, but I didn't want to tell the manager. I figured that since the fibrillations can stop as quickly as they start and since they really don't bother me unless they go on for a very long time, there was no sense in coming out of the game.

I played a couple of innings with my heart racing and stopping, and in the seventh, with us ahead, 7-6, Wayne Comer smacked a home run to tie the score. While I was snapping out of my crouch, the fibrillations stopped. Maybe it was the sudden movement—or the emotional shock of seeing Wayne's second home run in three days.

Comer had six hits against us in this series. He's proof

that expansion has hurt us. He was a utility outfielder for us last year—maybe the twenty-third or twenty-fourth most important guy on the roster. But he contributed. To win a pennant, the twenty-third or twenty-fourth guy on your club has to be better than the twenty-third or twenty-fourth guy on the other clubs, and Comer was probably the best twenty-third or twenty-fourth man in the league.

Earl Wilson was our starting pitcher today, and after he gave up six runs in five innings, the manager took him out. Earl thought he should have stayed in. He figured that he was getting himself back together and since the game was close, he could come on and maybe finish strong. I was inclined to agree with him, but Mayo wasn't, so the bullpen guys got some work and, finally, Pat Dobson ended up giving them their eighth run and getting beat.

Afterward, Wilson was teed off at himself and the world. Earl takes defeat about as hard as anybody in baseball. You have to understand him. After he's been knocked out or lost a game, don't talk to him. He says things then that he doesn't really mean.

I walked into a bar tonight, and Wilson and Gates Brown and McLain and Jim Price and a couple of other guys were already there. Everybody was standing at the bar—except Earl. He was sitting alone at a table. Gates bought a drink and went over and asked Earl if he wanted one, too. Earl just grumbled, "Arrrh . . . naah, don' wanna drink." Gates did a double take. He looked at Earl and said, "It must be great to be a star. When you're a scrub and you just play a little bit, you got to be nice to everybody. When you're a star, then you can walk around mad at everybody all the time."

Gates was hurt, but what we have to realize is we're all individuals. We're all different. Earl, Gates, Denny and, certainly, me.

June 2

We're in the only major-league suburb—Anaheim, California—and even though we're not allowed to go swimming or even lounge around the hotel in bathing suits—the club thinks it would be bad for our image—I like this place. I like it because I am the most successful suburban hitter in baseball.

I was reading the California Angels' yearbook before the game tonight, and I saw that I had both the highest batting average and the most RBIs of any visiting player in the four-year history of the Anaheim stadium.

The knowledge inspired me in batting practice—I hit the ball tremendously—but it didn't do me any good in the game. We lost, 3-1, and I didn't get a hit.

I'm in a slump. I'm not driving in any runs. I've been batting eighth in the order lately, and as long as I stay there, I'm afraid I won't drive in many runs. I have a mental block about batting eighth because I know that with the pitcher following me in the order I'm not going to see many good pitches to hit. Last year I was sixth in the American League in RBIs, but I didn't bat eighth last year.

A story appeared in the *Detroit News* today—by a writer named Watson Spoelstra—saying that Mayo had no imagination, that Jim Campbell wasn't making any trades to help the ball club, and—most infuriating—that an "unidentified" Tiger had said we had no chance to catch Baltimore. *What* player said that? Did *any* player say that?

The Detroit newspapers were on strike during much of last season, and I swear it helped the club. We didn't have any of this ridiculous divisive gossip floating around. Sure, baseball writers want to write inside stories, and sometimes they do, but they can get as sloppy with their facts as we can ever get on the field.

"I've made every effort to make trades," Jim Campbell said to me tonight. "If that man only knew the efforts I've made to get Jim Fregosi . . . but he doesn't know what's going on."

Jim said he didn't mind so much the personal attack on him, or on Mayo, but the "unidentified" player really got to him. "If it's true," Jim said, "and the player doesn't have enough guts to say it publicly, then he ought not to be saying it for print at all. I'd like to find that guy and crucify him from end to end." I'd like to find him, too—if he exists.

I don't believe any of my teammates would say that— not the way we've been playing lately. Even with two defeats in a row, we've won thirteen of our last eighteen games. We're five games over .500 now, 25-20, and we're seven and a half games behind the Baltimore Orioles, who are 35-15. They're not going to keep playing .700 ball; no one has in fifteen years. We've got four full months to go—117 games—and if we keep playing good ball, we're going to catch the Orioles.

June 3

With Lolich missing another start, we lost our third in a row tonight and I almost lost my hotel room. My roomie, Square Deal Sparma, is running short on cash again— that $100 couldn't last forever—and when he heard a salesman moaning in the hotel lobby that he couldn't find a room in Anaheim, Joe offered to sell ours. "Only ten bucks for the night," Sparma said. Joe didn't even consult me. I think we could've gotten more.

June 4

My roomie pitched today. Joe started the game and pitched six innings, really battling out of jams, and came out with a 4-2 lead. It was a gutsy effort and the manager, who usually isn't even on speaking terms with Joe, made a special trip over to him when he came out, the first time he's talked to Joe in days, and said, "Nice going. That was a hell of an effort. That's the way to stay with it."

The Angels tied up the game, 4-4, and in the tenth inning I came up against Hoyt Wilhelm with runners on base and a few things on my mind. I wanted to win a game for us because we were going bad. I wanted to do it against Wilhelm because he'd just walked Cash intentionally to pitch to me. And I wanted to do it against Wilhelm for another reason.

The other reason was personal—a matter of personal pride. Last February, Wilhelm and I played in a golf tournament together. We played in the same foursome, and before we began, we had a little conversation. We talked about baseball and we talked about our golf games. To hear Wilhelm talk, his golf game wasn't in the same league with mine. So he talked me into spotting him a few strokes, and we made a small bet on the round. Well, I gave him more strokes than I should have and he won five dollars from me. It wasn't the five dollars I minded losing, not at all. It was a matter of pride. My daddy always told me that the important thing was not how well you played golf but how well you wagered on the first tee. That day with Wilhelm, I'm afraid I disappointed my daddy, so I told Hoyt afterward that one of these days I was going to get even.

When you hit against Wilhelm's knuckle ball, you should try to tap the pitch to the opposite field. I did it tonight. I poked a single into right field and knocked in a run, and we won the game. When I got down to first base, I looked at the pitcher's mound and yelled over to Hoyt. "Hey," I said, "that's for the five bucks you took from me on the golf course back in February."

I'd rather lose five bucks to Wilhelm on the golf course or bat against him than catch him. Catching a knuckle-ball pitcher is probably the hardest thing in the world. You never know what a knuckle ball is going to do. Sometimes it sinks, sometimes it shoots straight in, sometimes it cracks you right in the mask. The first year I came up with the Tigers, we had a pitcher who was playing around with a knuckle ball—Tom Sturdivant. The first time I caught a game on national television, Sturdivant was pitching for us. Twice, his knuckle balls hit me in the protective cup instead of in the glove. Right there on national TV.

The first All-Star Game I ever played in I caught a knuckle-ball pitcher, too. Eddie Fisher. It was one of the most frightening experiences I've ever gone through. I said a few prayers that day.

June 5

We left Los Angeles today, the end of our million-dollar road trip. It was funny playing the Angels without Bill Rigney managing them. Bill was always a colorful guy, a lot of fun to be around. I remember one time we were playing the Angels and beating them something like 12-0 or 14-0 in about the sixth inning. We'd just hit a couple of tremendous home runs and now Cash was coming to bat. Norman got set in the batter's box, and just as the pitcher was about to deliver the ball, Rigney came racing out of the dugout and called time out. But instead of walking out to talk to his pitcher, or his catcher, he came right to home plate, toward Norman.

Norman was a little dumbfounded as Rigney came toward him, especially when Rigney said what he wanted to do was get a look at the ball. The umpire was a little dumbfounded, too. "What do you want to see the ball for?" the ump asked.

"I just want to check," Rigney said, "to make sure these are the same balls my team is trying to hit."

The new manager is Lefty Phillips. He's a former pitching coach, a former pitcher. Pitchers don't usually become managers, which is a bit strange since about seventy-five percent of this game on any given day is pitching. I guess people figure that a pitcher isn't familiar enough with batting to know how to handle that end of the game.

We notice one thing different already with Phillips in there instead of Rigney. Phillips pulls his pitchers out of the game a heck of a lot quicker than Rigney did. A boy gets in trouble and Phillips jumps out there right away. He walks real slow, with his head down—like a relief pitcher does when he comes plodding in from the bullpen—and he gets the man out of there right away.

We were talking about Rigney and Phillips on the plane. Today was an off-day, but we spent most of it in Los Angeles, got an afternoon flight out, and didn't get home to Detroit until 9:15 at night. Usually, we'll fly out right after the game, even if it's very late and get to spend some more time at home. I prefer that. I'd rather fly all night and get home at six o'clock in the morning than do what we did today. But I guess the club couldn't make different flight arrangements. Anyway, I'm dragging. Real tired. And my arm is killing me. I think I'm going to have to get a cortisone injection in my shoulder —or, at the least, I'll have to get some ultra-sound treatment.

June 6

We're back in Detroit finally, after eleven days on the road, and statistically, I had a good game tonight. I got a home run and a single, and I threw out the only guy who tried to steal on me.

But I know I didn't play well. I was dragging. The 25,000 people who paid to watch me play were cheated. After the long flight from Los Angeles yesterday, I had no energy left. Each time I ran down to first base, backing up plays, I had to walk back to home plate to catch my breath. I had a knot in my shoulder, and every time I threw, I felt like I had a toothache in my arm.

The last time I hit, my bat, which weighs about thirty-four ounces, felt like eighty ounces in my hand. A lot of the guys were exhausted. Oakland beat us, our fourth defeat in five games.

June 7

Five days ago, after he pitched against the Angels, Denny McLain went home to Detroit. He said he had to get his teeth fixed and his arm treated. Mayo gave him permission, which didn't exactly please the rest of us who had to stay on the West Coast. We all would have liked to go home early.

Denny was kind enough to show up for today's game, but he worked only an hour and fifty-one minutes. By then, he had shut out Oakland, a real breeze. Denny is unbelievable. He can make this game look so ridiculously easy.

The game was even easy for me. Suddenly, my arm felt loose, and so did I.

June 8

The weather was ugly this morning, rainy and gloomy, but I figured we'd play. We don't usually postpone Sunday games unless there's a hurricane; a lot of people come in from out of state, and they'd rather sit through a drizzle than go home without seeing a game. And the club would just as soon collect their ticket money.

I reached the stadium at eleven this morning, and the attendant in the parking lot told me the game had been postponed. I couldn't believe it. Then I realized that today was "Bat Day," free bats for all the youngsters at the game. The management didn't want to let all the people in, give away a bunch of bats, and risk having to give everyone a rain check. The youngsters sure wouldn't have given their bats back.

Whatever the financial reasoning, I was glad to get a day off. I'd heard on the radio that it wasn't raining up north. I wasn't due at the park again until 3 P.M. tomorrow, so I called my wife and told her that if she could pack up quickly, I'd drive her and my daughters up to our lake house. She said sure, and I drove home, packed the kids in the back of the station wagon with their little television set, and took off for the north. About a hundred miles out of Detroit, we hit a clear, blue sky.

I went sailing this afternoon and only whomped myself in the head with the boom twice. We'll have to leave at noon tomorrow to get back to Detroit by three, which means I'll have spent six out of twenty-seven hours driving. I don't care. This is a lot better than sitting in the house, watching the rain, and waiting for the next baseball game to come.

June 9

Mickey Lolich came back tonight, struck out sixteen Seattle batters to tie his own team record, and gave up only one run in nine innings. But still we lost. We lost in the tenth inning. We had a chance to win in the bottom of the ninth, with the bases loaded and Gates Brown, our most successful pinch hitter last year, batting for Lolich. This isn't last year. Gates didn't come through.

John Fetzer, our owner, was at the game, and he was philosophical about the troubles we've been having. "When you're successful like we were last year," he told me, "it changes your life. In a lot of respects, failure is easier to cope with. You're all finding that out because your lives are completely different than they were last year at this time. You've had a lot of things come your way, a lot of good things, and a lot of new pressures."

I told Mr. Fetzer that my life had never been more complicated, that instead of having a simple life, concerned only with baseball, I now had business constantly on my mind, too. It's tough coping with everything, learning perspective, sorting through the obligations, and establishing priorities.

June 10

As I was going out to batting practice before we beat Seattle tonight, the manager came up and asked how my arm was. "I can play," I said.

"Well, I know it's bothering you," Mayo said. "Take the night off."

I figured that was fair enough until, a few minutes later, I picked up the first edition of the *Detroit Free Press* and saw a story that quoted Mayo as saying he was going to bench me because I wasn't driving in any runs. I was upset for two reasons. First, there's no way in the world you're going to drive in any runs batting eighth. Second, I want to know why Mayo gave me one reason for the night off and gave a newspaperman another.

June 11

When I got to the park today, I saw that my name wasn't listed in the starting lineup for the second straight day. I went out, took batting practice, then warmed up some pitchers—to show Mayo, I guess, that although my arm hurt, it was strong enough for me to play. Then I went to his office. "Yesterday you told me to my face that I wasn't playing because of my arm," I said to the manager. "Then I read in the paper that you said you were benching me because I wasn't driving in any runs."

"Who wrote that?" he said.

"George Cantor," I said.

"I never said that to him," Mayo said.

"Well, I'll give you the benefit of the doubt," I said. "But I want you to know that it doesn't tee me off that you're not playing me; you're writing the lineup and that's your decision. But for you to tell me one thing and then for me to read a completely different thing in the paper, that tees me off. And the other thing that bothers me was your saying I wasn't driving in any runs. You know as well as I do that you're not going to drive in any runs batting eighth."

"Aah, don't worry," Mayo said. "I'll give you tonight off. And I won't play you in the exhibition game in Toledo tomorrow. That'll be three nights off. By Friday, your arm'll be strong. You'll have some rest on it and maybe you'll be back to where the injury's not bothering you."

"Okay," I said. When I walked out the door, I felt a lot better than I had on my way to the park.

A little while later, Mayo called a team meeting and chewed out the whole club. We've been messing up a lot of signs lately (the other day one of our batters completely missed a hit-and-run sign, and the runner was thrown out at second easily), and that was on Mayo's mind. "Boys," he said, "the next sign that's missed will cost $25. It'll be $50 the second offense and it'll build up. The signs aren't that difficult. When I see guys that are pretty intelligent missing 'em, then I know it's lack of concentration. Maybe the fines'll make you concentrate. We can't afford mistakes.

"And another thing. On the last road trip, we had some problems with curfew violations. There'll be no more of that. The next time anyone's caught out after curfew, it's going to be a $1,000 fine. Not $200, not $500, but $1,000. I want you in when I tell you to be in. A few hundred dollars may not mean much to you guys, but you'll have trouble explaining at home why $1,000 is missing from your paycheck."

In the game, Mickey Stanley, leading off, popped up. From out in the bullpen, where I was sitting, we couldn't see what was going on, but we heard a lot of noise—a lot of cracking and banging—after he went back to the bench, and we saw everybody looking into the dugout. What happened, we found out later, was that Mickey, who hasn't been hitting too well, had completely destroyed the bat rack.

Out in the bullpen with Radatz, Dobson, and McMahon for the second night in a row, I was accepted as a regular. I was even invited to eat from the stock of food they take down there. They're not allowed to take ice cream or hot dogs or anything heavy into the bullpen, but they can bring in little snacks. I took an inventory last night and for eleven guys, they had four Payday bars, three Clark bars, eighteen salami sticks, ten pieces of bubble gum, four packs of Doublemint gum, three Butterfinger bars, three Planters Peanut bars, four bags of peanuts, and four Hershey bars. They eat like that every night. Everything's usually gone by about the fourth inning. I guess it's a good way to take care of some of your nervous energy.

McLain started for us against Seattle and pitched well considering he had a 102-degree temperature and looked white as a sheet in the trainer's room before the game. In the ninth, with the score, 2-2, I was called to pinch-hit and had a chance to be a hero. I blew the chance. I came in cold—I usually like to know what the pitcher I'm facing has been throwing—took a couple of good swings, and popped out.

Seattle got a run in the tenth to go ahead, 3-2, but in the bottom of the inning. Cash, Kaline, Northrup, and my replacement, Jim Price, came up with hits and we won, 4-3. A Tiger Finish. I'd almost forgotten what they looked like.

We're six games over .500 for the first time this season. But guess what? Baltimore won, too.

June 12

We played an exhibition in Toledo tonight, mostly to draw a $20,000 gate for our top farm club, and even though the game didn't mean anything to us, we had a busy evening.

First, before the game, Al Kaline couldn't find his sanitary hose, the white socks we wear under our long socks. "Hey," Kaline yelled to the clubhouse man, "you got any undersocks?"

"Undersocks?" said one of the younger guys. "What's that?"

"You aren't old enough to know," said Kaline. "That's what we called sanitary socks back in the mid-fifties."

The rest of us took a vote right then and decided, from now on, we'd call sanitary hose "undersocks" so that the veterans like Kaline and Cash wouldn't feel so old.

Second, Jim Price sprained his ankle before the game, and I lost my night off. Mayo was willing to let Dave Campbell catch and put me at first base, but I insisted on catching. Suppose Dave had a good game? I might never get back behind the plate.

Third, in the ninth inning, with Toledo leading, 5-4, Dick McAuliffe hit into a double play to end the game, and Jim Northrup promptly congratulated him for getting it finished. We didn't take the defeat too hard.

The star of the game was a young fellow who's been hitting about .360 for Toledo, a guy named Ike Brown. Mayo's thinking of bringing him up to give us some right-handed pinch-hitting and some infield help. Mayo told us to pitch carefully to him, to really test him.

The first time Ike came up, I said, "Have a good night because the big man is looking at you." He hit a breaking ball for a home run. Later, Ike got another hit on a breaking ball, and in the seventh inning, when he came up again, Mayo told us to try fast balls on the inside. Ike got another hit, driving in the two runs that won the game. I think he'll be joining us soon.

Fred Lasher was the losing pitcher for us, and at one point he decided to experiment with a knuckler. I don't think Lasher ought to be experimenting with a knuckler, and I don't particularly like to catch one, so I told the batter it was coming. He got a base hit. Then he told Lasher I'd told him the pitch was coming.

Fred was pretty unhappy with me, but I didn't care. I still had all five fingers on my right hand.

Lasher's kind of a strange guy. He doesn't always have too much confidence in himself. When he gives up a home run, he'll go around after the game, asking half a dozen guys whether they think he threw the right pitch. The more he shows his insecurity about his pitching, the more we kid him about it. He's always the butt of jokes. Tonight, a bunch of the guys were calling him The Giant Hamster and telling him that Mud Hens, the nickname of the Toledo team, weren't supposed to eat hamsters. Lasher took most of the abuse pretty good-naturedly. My roommate says that if the guys agitated him the way they agitate Fred, he'd punch somebody in the nose.

June 13

My roomie's got an ESP thing. Every now and then, he'll wake up on a morning he's supposed to pitch and say, "I've got a good feeling. I know we're going to win." Joe doesn't get this feeling too often, but every time he does—every single time—we win.

"I've got a good feeling," Sparma said this morning in the Muehlebach Hotel in Kansas City. Tonight, he shut out the Royals, 6-0.

Joe had a really good breaking ball, really snapping it to me, and fine control; he walked only two men.

It was a good night for our room. I moved up to seventh

in the batting order, displacing Tommy Matchick, who wasn't too happy about sliding back to eighth. I didn't do much tonight, but now that I'm up to seventh, I think I'll start driving in some runs. Maybe I can work myself up to sixth or fifth, the slots I hit in most of the time last year.

After the game, some of the guys were wondering whether Mayo really was serious about his new curfew —two and a half hours after the finish of a night game, instead of two and a half hours after the bus gets back to the hotel. A few of us asked Jim Price, our player representative, to double-check with Mayo.

Jim phrased the question very delicately—Mayo hasn't been in a good mood lately—and almost got his head bitten off. Mayo told him that two and a half hours after the game meant one hundred and fifty minutes after the final out.

In the clubhouse, everybody was yelling at everybody else to shave and shower quickly because we didn't have much time to get back to the hotel and find a place to eat dinner.

Half an hour after midnight, two and a half hours after the third out, Mayo started calling our hotel rooms, checking on everybody. He called Mickey Stanley and said, "Is your roommate there?"

"Northrup's asleep," Mickey said. Northrup was sitting in a little alcove in the hallway, talking with Radatz, Campbell, Woods, Horton, Sparma, and me.

"Okay," Mayo said. "I'll take your word for it."

Then Mayo rang my room. I answered. "Is Joe there?" the manager said.

"He's asleep," I said. I started to giggle.

"I don't believe you," said Mayo. "Let me talk to him." Joe got on the phone.

I'm glad that he and the manager are talking again.

June 14

We were rained out today, so we watched Baltimore play Chicago on network television. On the pregame TV show, Mickey Mantle said Baltimore was probably the strongest team in either the American or the National League and that he was picking the Orioles to win the pennant. I disagree with him.

But I've got to admit the Orioles are incredible. Today, when Paul Blair squared around to bunt, Tommy John, the Chicago pitcher, threw the ball in front of the plate and right by the catcher. So, instead of sacrificing an out to advance a runner one base, the Orioles moved the runner two bases and didn't even give up an out. It's funny, but that's the way things went for us last year.

I got so frustrated watching that, in the fourth inning, with Baltimore ahead, 7-2, I turned off the television set.

June 15

I'm on the road so much I sent my wife a Father's Day card today. I phoned Pat, too, wished her a happy Father's Day, and told her to go out and buy herself a Father's Day present.

We beat Kansas City today, 7-0, a two-hitter for Earl Wilson, his strongest game of the year.

Before the game, I chatted with Joe Foy, the Royals' third baseman, and Pat Kelly, their rookie center fielder. Kelly's third in the league in stolen bases, and Foy said to me, "This man's going to steal a couple on you today. He's got something on you."

"He wouldn't be getting any cherry," I said. But I was on guard. When Kelly got a double, I was just waiting for him to go. And he did, too. He didn't get a very good jump, I made a good throw for a change, and we got him.

In the eighth inning, Kelly walked, but by then we were ahead, 7-0, and were concentrating only on getting batters out, not on holding runners on. "Hey, no fair try-ing now," I hollered. "It doesn't count if you steal now." He didn't try.

I felt pretty good today. I was throwing okay and I got a hit and a walk. Jim Northrup got the big hit for us, a three-run homer, and Dick McAuliffe had the best day of all.

During batting practice, Mac had mentioned he'd had a tough time sleeping last night and wasn't feeling too good. My roomie, Square Deal ESP, said, "Mac, I know you're going to have a good day today. Something just tells me you're going to go three for five."

Mac got three hits his first four times up, then struck out. He came back to the dugout and walked over to the water cooler where Joe and I were sitting. "That strikeout was your fault, Sparma," he said, "because you told me I was going to go three for five and you jinxed me." He was actually angry. He could've at least thanked Joe for the three hits.

Joe and Mac are always agitating each other. My roomie keeps saying that Mac's a pretty good ballplayer, but what keeps him from being great is the fact that he's half-Italian and half-Irish. It's the Irish half, Joe tells Mac, that holds him back.

There's a lot of that kind of kidding around in baseball. I realize baseball's no utopia in religious and racial rela-tions, but I think the game's a little ahead of most of society. Among my teammates, at least, there's little paranoia, little looking behind an absurd joke for a deep-rooted, hidden prejudice. When we traded Ron Woods to the Yankees for Tom Tresh today, Norm Cash, a white Texas country boy, could say to Earl Wilson, a proud, tough black man, "Hey, I thought that was a great trade —when you get one white guy for one colored guy even up." Everybody was able to laugh.

We got in just the one trade before the June 15 mid-night deadline. It wasn't as important a trade as we would have liked, but it's going to help us. Woods has a chance to be a good major-league ballplayer, but as a backup guy for Horton, he wasn't terribly valuable to our club. Tresh, with his experience and versatility—he can play short, second, third, and the outfield—can help us immediately. He's not hitting well, but Yankee Stadium is a tough park if you're not a pull hitter. Besides, when Wally Moses was batting coach for the Yankees, Tom hit .279 one year, with twenty-six homers and seventy-four RBIs.

Tom joined us today, and he's happy to be here. He's from a suburb of Detroit and he has a home up north, near mine. "I don't want to leave New York," he told the Yankees a few weeks ago, "but if you're going to trade me, if there's any way that you can get me to Detroit, I'd really appreciate it." Tom told me the Yankees probably could've traded him for other people on other clubs, but they had some feelings for his wishes. The Yankees are a class organization.

Tom told me this on the plane tonight, flying from Kansas City to New York for a five-game series with the Yankees. I made sure we sat together so we could discuss the things a catcher always wants to know when you get a guy from another team. We talked about how the Yankee hitters have been swinging lately, about individual strengths and weaknesses. I asked him if the Yankees were stealing any of my signs or if any of our players were tipping off when they were going to swing or take or steal. Of course, with Woods over there, we'll have to change our signs. That can't hurt us; our own guys—according to Mayo—hadn't learned the signs yet, anyway.

This season, so far, is hard to believe. We just took two in a row from Kansas City—and lost ground to Baltimore. The Orioles swept four from Chicago. We're eight games over .500 now, not far off the pace I wanted to see us set and not far behind the pace we were setting at this time last year. But we're nine full games behind Baltimore. Those guys are already twenty-six games over .500. I guess I've got to revise my preseason estimate that twenty-eight games over .500 would win our division. But I still think that thirty-four games over .500— 98—64 for the season—will be good enough to win.

Baltimore's climbing toward that level fast, and it looks like the only club that can slow them down is us. Between now and the All-Star break in Mid-July, we play them eight times. If we can win six of those eight, we'll be in good shape. We'll have them looking over their shoulders.

June 16

As I got on the bus to Yankee Stadium today, I heard that Dick Radatz had been sold to Montreal. I was surprised. I thought he'd been pitching well, better than anybody else in the bullpen lately.

Then John Sain, our pitching coach, came on the bus and sat down next to me. Before I could ask him about Radatz, John turned to me and said, "I hear Radatz was traded. That true?"

I nodded.

"They get a player for him?" John said. "Or just money?"

"Just money, I guess," I said.

Suddenly, I realized this was the pitching coach asking me these questions. How come he hadn't been consulted on the deal? Or even told about it? He'd been working hard with Radatz and had helped bring him around. John seemed disturbed. According to him, the manager and general manager hadn't asked him for his recommendation before dealing Radatz.

Dave Campbell—C. A. Boatride—was gone, too, down to the minors. To replace Dave and Radatz, we brought up Tom Timmerman, a pitcher, and Ike Brown, the hitter, from Toledo. Ike caught the bus to the stadium, carrying his Toledo duffel bag with his bat taped to it. "Have bat, can hit, will travel," I thought. Everybody seemed happy to see him. He has the potential to help us a lot.

A third man joined the team today. Denny McLain. He just spent a few days in the hospital with food poisoning —he shouldn't play in clubs that serve that kind of food —but he showed up to pitch today. And he beat the Yankees, 3-2.

Kaline hit a two-run home run for our margin of victory, but after the game, he was all alone at his locker while the writers surrounded Denny. "Hey, Al," one of the writers called to him. "Maybe you didn't hit any home run. Maybe it was just part of our imagination, and that's why nobody wants to talk to you."

"No," Al said, loud enough to needle McLain, "It's just that I'm around all the time. You don't get a chance to talk to Denny much."

Then Don McMahon, our quiet relief pitcher, of all people, called to McLain, "Hey, Denny. Nice job. See you next weekend."

"Hey, Nanook," I shouted to McMahon. We call him Nanook because when he goes to the bullpen, he bundles up like an Eskimo. "Don't go popping off and starting trouble."

"Okay," McMahon said. "If the man can win for us, I'll leave him alone."

McMahon's a professional—in his thirteenth big-league season—with a professional attitude, and I've got to agree with him. Denny is a winner. A lot of guys on the club wish we had four guys like Denny who'd show up every fourth day and win twenty games. He'd go to the bank fat every winter.

But, sometimes, he really bugs me. Like today, in the ninth inning, we were ahead, 3-1, with two men out, a man on second and Gene Michael at bat. Michael's not a particularly tough hitter, which means he's the kind of guy Denny doesn't bear down on.

Mayo came out to the mound. "Throw the ball up on this guy," the manager said. "Up and in. You've been throwing him low stuff and he's been hitting it."

"Sure, sure," Denny said. Then he winked. "I'm going to throw the ball down, across the middle. He can't hit it."

"This isn't funny," Mayo said.

"Right," Denny said. He winked again.

Mayo left the mound, I went back behind the plate and Denny threw his first pitch down low. Michael banged out a base hit, driving in their second run. Only Denny would do something like that—a little test to see if the manager was really right.

Denny's incredible. And so's his record. He's 10-5 now, and he could be headed for another thirty-victory season. They don't make many like Denny—fortunately for my sanity and our opponents' batting averages.

After the game tonight, I went to the Chateau Madrid, a nightclub I enjoy, and the owner, Danny Lopez, invited me to join him and some other people at his table. The other people included Albert Shanker, the president of the teachers' union in New York, and Joseph Monserrat, the president of the Board of Education.

"These guys have been battling for days," Lopez told me. "They keep talking settlements and strikes. They can't think about anything else. Let's talk baseball, for a change."

We talked baseball for a while, and Shanker and Monserrat both knew quite a bit about the game. We had a good time—Danny Lopez said I had them more relaxed than they'd been in weeks—and I hated to leave to beat curfew. But I couldn't quite imagine me telling the manager, "Mayo, how can you fine me a thousand dollars? I was just trying to help settle the school strike in New York."

June 17

We swept a doubleheader from the Yankees today, and now we've got a seven-game winning streak going and we're eleven games over .500. I batted eighth in the first game and drove in a run—with a home run. Mayo promoted me to the fourth spot in the second game, and I went hitless, didn't even get the ball out of the infield. That's the kind of year I'm having. I get an opportunity, and I don't do anything about it.

Ike Brown started at third base for us in the second game, and his second time up he got his first major-league hit—a home run. We gave him the silent treatment. He came rushing in, feeling good and expecting to be congratulated, and we just sat there, as if nothing had happened. He got halfway down the bench, past all those frozen faces, then turned on us. "Okay, you guys," he said. Before he could finish, we were all up pounding him, giving him some skin.

Ike's next time up, the first pitch came at his head and knocked him on his tail. He got up, not at all intimidated, and banged a base hit through the middle. He's going to be all right.

With Ike and with Tom Tresh, who played shortstop in the first game and got a couple of hits, we have some maneuverability now. For shortstop we've got Stanley, Tresh, Dick Tracewski, and McAuliffe. For second and third, we've got Tresh, McAuliffe, Tracewski, Ike Brown, Wert, and Matchick. For the outfield, we have Stanley, Tresh, Horton, Gates Brown, Kaline, and Northrup. Cash can play first, and I can, and Kaline and Northrup, too. We're getting stronger.

After the second game, Sparma and I went over to Bachelors III, Joe Namath's place, to see all the Mafia people who supposedly hang around there. We saw mostly athletes—Tom Keating, the tackle for the Oakland Raiders; E. J. Holub, the center for the Kansas City

Chiefs; Namath, and Joe Pepitone of the Yankees. Pepitone hasn't played against us these last three games; he's had a strep throat. That's fine with me. I'll tell you: I'd rather buy Joe Pepitone a drink any time than have to throw him a pitch.

June 18

My roomie pitched today, and he was beating the Yankees, 2-1, in the bottom of the seventh inning. Then he walked two guys, and Mayo lifted him. Joe wasn't too happy.

I was sitting on the bench, resting again, and John Sain turned to me. "It's a little rough being out there like Joe," John said, "knowing the manager doesn't have any confidence in you."

I know Sparma just isn't as loose and as confident as he ought to be.

My own confidence is a little rocky, too. Before the game, Mayo told me I probably needed a rest after catching the doubleheader last night. "Come on, Mayo," I said. "Tell it like it is." I was smiling, not angry. "Don't tell me you're not playing me 'cause I'm tired. It's probably 'cause I went oh-for-four in the second game and didn't swing the bat too good, and Price is swinging better. Just tell me straight out the other guy's doing a better job."

"That's got nothing to do with it," Mayo said, but he didn't fully convince me.

I pinch-hit late in the game against Steve Hamilton, a gangly, funny-looking guy, and he threw me a funny-looking pitch. He came halfway through his motion, stopped as if he'd been tripped, then floated the ball up out of a tangle of falling body motion and flapping arms. I backed out and started laughing. I didn't know if he'd tripped or what. "Was that a mistake?" I asked their catcher. "Or did he do it intentionally?"

"On purpose," the catcher said. "That's Steve's hesitation pitch."

I got back in the batter's box and I couldn't stop laughing. I had to step out, get some resin on my hands, and try to get my concentration back. Then I hit a normal pitch, a good drive that their left fielder caught. I guess the hesitation pitch did its job; it sure got me off balance.

We lost the game. Our relief pitchers didn't help Sparma at all. They gave up three runs, and our winning streak ended. I guess I'm going to have to give up the green cowboy hat I've been wearing here. I borrowed it from the Knox Hat Shop in the Roosevelt Hotel, our headquarters in New York, and I was going to keep wearing it as long as our winning streak lasted—and as long as I could stand the abuse. Guys were saying I looked either like a plantation owner or a midnight cowboy.

Joe Pepitone of the Yankees cracked up when he saw my hat, but he's no one to talk. We always kid Pepi about his bouffant hairdo. His hair sticks out in back, and today, during batting practice, I picked up a large chunk of dead turf and handed it to Cash. "Hey, Norman," I said. "Stick this under your cap, and you'll look like Pepitone."

Norm put it on, then shouted, "Pepi, Pepi, how do you like my hairpiece?"

Guess what?

The Orioles won today. We've won seven of eight, and we're still eight and a half games out of first place.

June 19

Before the game at Yankee Stadium tonight, I noticed that Ike Brown, who had the locker next to mine, was putting on a pair of baseball shoes that were falling apart. "I got a new pair the same size as yours," I said. "Take 'em."

"How much you want for them?" Ike said.

"Nothing," I said. "I've got a contract with Wilson, and they give 'em to me. Just take 'em."

"You're kidding."

Ike wore the shoes in batting practice and, just before the game, I walked up to him. "Ike," I said, "I'm not superstitious, but what did you hit at Toledo?"

"Oh, .364, .365," he said.

"Man," I said, "if I hit .365 anywhere, there ain't nothing I'd change."

Ike kind of smiled, and later, his first time up, he beat out an infield hit and scored a run. When he came back to the dugout, I looked over at him and, sure enough, he'd put on his old shoes. "I ain't superstitious, either," he said, "but I'm not taking any chances."

If I were hitting the way Ike's been hitting, I'd eat the same food every meal.

I did more talking during the game than hitting—arguing with the plate umpire, Bill Haller, who must've had something in his eye. We jawed at each other all night— I never turned around, but he knew who I was talking to —and one time, when Pepitone was hitting, Joe stepped out of the batter's box and said, "If you guys are going to argue, just do it without me. I'm not hitting while you're arguing."

We lost the game. Baltimore won. Par for the course.

Afterward, at LaGuardia Airport, waiting for our charter plane, a young United Air Lines mechanic walked over to Northrup, Kaline, and me, and asked us if the Tigers ever held tryout camps. He said he was twenty years old, but I thought he looked a little older.

"What do scouts look for?" he asked.

"Natural ability," I said. "The ability to swing the bat and coordination. And size."

He wasn't too big.

"You playing in any regular league?" I said.

He used to, he said, but he wasn't this year because of

his job. He said he felt certain he could make it in the minor leagues because he had some friends playing who weren't any better than him.

Just then, Wally Moses walked out. "Ask him," I told the mechanic. "He's signed a lot of kids, and he's worked in the minor leagues. He knows the business."

I introduced Wally, and he asked the fellow what position he played. The kid said he played second base and could run good.

"You think you could play in the major leagues?" Wally said.

The kid paused. "Well," he said, "I don't know."

Just his hesitation made Wally smile. Wally's a blunt guy and, as soon as the kid hesitated, Wally said, "Listen, kid, if you even think you can't make it in the major leagues, then there's no use getting involved in this game."

"I know I can play in the minor leagues," the kid said.

"No future in that," Wally said. "You got a good job here. Stay on it."

"I don't like the job," he said. "My hands get too greasy."

"You know," Kaline said, "when you get finished with your job, you can always wipe the grease off. You can't wipe off those oh-for-fours and those boos."

"I'd still like to go play in the minor leagues even if I can't play in the majors," the kid said. He really didn't have a clue what baseball life is all about. "Yeah," he said, "I'd like to go down to the minors and play a couple of years, but I'm making ten thousand dollars a year here. I wouldn't play in the minors unless they could guarantee me a raise in pay."

We all looked at each other. "Hey, friend," I said, "you better stay right here. We've got two boys that just joined the club—one named Ike Brown and a boy named Tom Timmerman—and they've been playing pro ball since 1960 and, son, they have yet to make $10,000 a year in this game."

"You're kidding me," he said.

"No," I said. "You've been believing what you read in the papers about this business of ours. It looks glamorous from the outside, but I guarantee you, unless you're right on top, it isn't as glamorous as you think. If you don't think you can be a star, then don't try it. Just work hard as a mechanic and don't worry about the grease on your hands."

June 20

We landed in Detroit in pouring rain about four o'clock this morning—our charter had been delayed at La-Guardia—and Jim Northrup, Al Kaline, and I hustled to the United Air Lines ticket counter. The three of us live in the same neighborhood, and we'd arranged for our wives to leave one car at the airport for us. The keys to Northrup's car were at the United counter, with a diagram showing where the car was parked.

We hitched a ride to our car on a United crew van, and three crewmen from a freight plane jumped on right after us. One of them said to another, "We've got a full day in Detroit. I wonder if the Tigers are in town."

"Yeah," I interrupted. "They're playing here tonight."

The guy looked up and recognized us. "What the hell are you guys doing here at this hour?" he said.

"Don't look for much of a game tonight," I said.

When we reached our car, lightning and thunder began, and Kaline and I admitted we were scared. "Don't worry," Northrup said. "A car's the safest place to be in the middle of a lightning storm."

"I've heard that," I told Kaline.

"Yeah," said Al. "Me, too. But it doesn't make me feel much better when that lightning flashes."

Just then, as we were driving through a heavily wooded area, a big bolt of lightning crashed down. "Get in the middle of the road, Northrup," I said, "in case one of those trees comes down." A friend of mine, a guy I used to caddy with, got killed on a golf course when lightning knocked a tree down on him. I've been afraid of lightning ever since.

We started talking about a former Baltimore Oriole who was so afraid of lightning he had a clause in his contract saying that, in the event of any lightning, he could leave the field and take the day off. The way things have been running for the Orioles this year, I bet that, if he were still playing, they wouldn't even see a drizzle all season.

We saw a Tiger Finish tonight—by the Washington Senators. They came from behind, then scored five runs in the tenth inning and beat us, 7-2, our third defeat in a row. The key play was a bad throw by Mickey Stanley on a double-play pivot in the tenth inning. It was a tough play—the base runner knocked him off balance—but some big drunk in the stands started screaming at Mickey and really abusing him.

The drunk was sitting right behind Mickey's wife and my stockbroker, Jerry LeVan. Jerry had once shut up a drunk who'd been sitting behind my wife and hollering at me, and he was ready to tell off this guy tonight. But Mickey's wife said, "Don't do anything. I understand, and I'd rather you didn't say anything."

I guess baseball wives have to get used to things like that. They can't have rabbit ears any more than their husbands can.

June 21

We played miserably today. We committed three playing errors and at least that many mental errors. We were so bad that, after the game, Kaline, sitting in the whirlpool sipping a beer, suddenly piped up, in a little boy's voice, "But, daddy, I saw a Tiger do that on television last Saturday."

Once, with the bases loaded and nobody out, Cash grounded to the shortstop, who threw to second, forcing Kaline. Then the second baseman threw wildly to first, so Cash kept running. As he approached second base, he saw Kaline getting up from his slide. Norm stopped, turned around, headed toward first, then remembered that Kaline must've been forced, turned around again and ran safely to second. Afterward in the locker room, someone said we should polish that play in the spring. "Right," Cash said, "and Kaline can be our second-base coach."

Northrup dropped a fly ball during the game, and later one of the guys, imitating Jim, held up his glove and slammed a ball into it, and everybody else shouted, "Clank!" We also imitated Cash losing a pop fly in the sun and Ike Brown swinging so hard he fell down on his follow-through.

We were able to laugh mostly because the Senators were even more miserable than us. Willie Horton batted in six runs, and we won, 9-5.

In the evening, I took my daughters to the drive-in theater to see *Peter Pan*.

I don't have many chances to be a father during the summer, so, whenever I can, I like to spend time with my kids. It's rough being the child of a ballplayer. I've seen players' sons who identify so closely with their fathers that when their fathers aren't hitting, the boys stay in their houses to avoid abuse from other kids.

Even with two girls, and an X on the way, I have troubles. When I just try to play in our yard with the girls, about fifty kids show up, all the boys swinging bats and throwing balls around. Within five minutes, I'm flooded by children, and my own daughters have retreated to the house, frightened because someone hit one of them in the back of the head with a bat or something like that.

June 22

We played an endless and deafening Bat Day double-header today. I was at the park for more than ten hours, with thousands of kids constantly pounding bats against the floor of the stadium and sometimes swinging them at each other; one kid actually belted a Tiger official with a bat.

Before we got started, Nellie Fox, the Senators' first-base coach, was telling me how much he liked the way Fred Lasher and Mike Kilkenny pitched. During the doubleheader, Lasher pitched and didn't get anybody out, and Kilkenny pitched and got knocked out. As Mike was leaving the game, I called down to Fox, "Hey, Nellie, you say *you* liked those guys—or *your hitters* liked those guys?"

Their hitters loved all our guys today. They belted our whole staff around and beat us both games. We've lost five out of six now, we're only seven games over .500 and we're twelve full games behind Baltimore. I'm really depressed.

The Orioles—I can hardly believe it—are already thirty-one games over .500. If they keep up their present pace, they will win more games than any team in the history of the game. They can't keep it up.

Can they?

June 23

Our pitchers, particularly our relief pitchers, have been getting ripped lately, but John Sain, who believes in positive thinking, hasn't lost faith in them. "I just thought of how to make a million dollars," he said to me before the game tonight.

"How?" I said.

"I'm going upstairs right now," he said, "and buy the pitching staff for what the newspapers think it's worth.

Then in a few weeks, when we get straightened out, I'll sell the staff back for what they think it's worth then."

John had his annual mid-season strategy talk with me today. "I don't like to criticize your signal-calling," he said, "but it's almost July now, and the hitters have gotten themselves into their grooves. Instead of challenging them with fast balls on 2-0 and 3-1 counts, the way we did in April and May, you've got to start calling more breaking pitches in those situations now. The hitters are organized now."

I tried John's strategy tonight against the Yankees—with a 2-0 count on Pepitone, I called for an off-speed pitch—and it worked. Pepitone was laying for the fast ball, and we fooled him.

We had a good night. Mike Kilkenny and Daryl Patterson pitched well in relief, and we came from behind and beat New York with a pinch-hit home run by the Big Guy, Jim Price. Cash saved the game for us with a great, diving play on a line drive in the ninth inning, and afterward, when he was having his knees patched up in the trainer's room, Norman said, "It's really something when I have to make a super catch to keep us twelve games back of first place."

June 24

Tom Tresh, Mickey Stanley, Don Wert, Gates Brown, and I went out on the field early this afternoon for some batting practice. We call ourselves "The Slumpers," and I think I've got a good chance to be captain of the club.

My batting average has dipped below .250 for the first time this year, and my RBI production has almost disappeared. On May 3, after four weeks of the season, I had thirteen RBIs, five of them from one game, the second game of the season. Now, more than seven weeks later, my total is up to only nineteen RBIs. At my current pace, I won't even drive in fifty runs the whole season; last year,

I had forty-six RBIs just in the first half of the season. I've got to get hot.

Wally Moses has been working with me again, getting me to open up my stance a little. The idea is that, first, I'll be able to get around better on inside pitches and, second, the new stance will free my left side, the side that determines bat speed for a right-handed hitter. I've been practicing at home, in front of a mirror, but so far it hasn't helped me much in a game. I've been thinking of mechanics and not attacking the ball spontaneously.

Denny McLain pitched tonight, and we got two runs for him in the first inning, a home run by Kaline that hit the top of the fence and bounced over and a home run by Horton.

In the eighth inning, we still had our two runs, and the Yankees had one, and McLain was riding the rest of us. "Hey, you guys, I'm pitching," he said. "We've got to score lots of runs. Let's go. I'm not used to working this hard." It's funny, but we usually do score a lot of runs for Denny.

I came to bat with men on first and second and one out, a good opportunity to drive in a run. "If you don't get a hit now," Denny yelled at me, "you deserve a kick in the ass. If you don't get a hit, don't bother putting on the equipment for the ninth inning."

I didn't get a hit (nor did Denny, following me). But I slipped on the catching equipment anyway, walked out to Denny after he made the third out, handed him his glove and hat and said, "Now's the time to call for Price if you want him."

Denny gave me one of his funny looks, then went and got three outs in a row, and wrapped up the victory.

June 25

After we beat the Yankees for the third straight night, a reporter asked me what I thought about our series in

Baltimore that starts the day after tomorrow. I gave the standard ballplayer's response. "The only thing on my mind now," I said, "is the fourth game with the Yankees. I'll worry about Baltimore when we get there."

Actually, like everybody else, I was watching the scoreboard tonight, rooting for the Senators to beat the Orioles. Joe Sparma and Earl Wilson bet a Coke on the game. Wilson bet on the Orioles. He bet another Coke that Denny wouldn't show up at the ball park before the fifth inning.

Guess what?

Sparma won both bets. The Orioles lost, and Denny showed up in the fourth inning.

We're using up our miracles.

June 26

We had our first miserably hot, humid night of the season tonight, and I lost eleven pounds, down from 217 to 206. Worse, we lost the ball game to the Yankees, 6-0.

We go to Baltimore tomorrow eleven and a half games behind the Orioles. They're now thirty-two games over .500.

Our record is 38-29. Last year, after sixty-seven games, we had a record of 43-24, and we were in first place by seven and a half games. If we had that exact same record this year, we'd still be six and a half games behind the Orioles.

We've got to win at least three out of four in Baltimore. We've got to.

June 27

Before the game tonight, the Baltimore pitchers were running in the outfield, practically sprinting in ninety-two-degree weather, and Norm Cash started agitating John Sain. "Hey, John," Cash yelled, "don't those guys know it's ninety-two degrees? What are they out there running for?"

Sain, of course, is not the leading advocate of running for pitchers; he says he wants his men to be ready to pitch nine innings, not run a mile.

Denny McLain, who is a real disciple of Sain's no-running policy, was standing next to John. Denny doesn't even like to hear people talk about running pitchers. He wasn't very happy with Cash's agitating.

Norman, to emphasize his needling, put his arm around Denny, but Denny had the last word. He brushed Norman's arm away. "Don't ever touch a superstar," he said.

Then the Orioles beat us, 4-1. They didn't exactly overpower us. Among their hits were a dinky ground ball by Dave Johnson that trickled over third base, a slow grounder by Ellie Hendricks that hit second base and bounced over Tom Tresh's glove, and a blooper that popped off Boog Powell's bat. Two of those three mighty blows drove in runs. For us, Kaline hit a couple of rockets; both of them produced double plays.

I had an ominous feeling watching the Orioles get all the good bounces. We were the luckiest team in the American League last year, and we won the 1968 pennant. The Boston Red Sox were the luckiest team in the American League two years ago, and they won the 1967 pennant. This year, Baltimore is getting a lot more than its share of the breaks.

June 28

After the 1966 All-Star Game in St. Louis, when the temperature hit 113 degrees on the field, someone asked Casey Stengel how he liked the new St. Louis ball park. "Sure holds the heat well," said Casey.

That was the most exhausting weather I ever played in. Baltimore won second prize today.

It was ninety-five degrees and humid when we got to the park, and our guys were obviously dragging. We weren't just fighting the weather. We'd played fifteen games in the last thirteen days in four different cities without a single day off. We'd played five night games in a row. Now, with an afternoon game, nobody'd had a chance to get any real rest. Cash and Kaline both admitted they couldn't remember the last time they'd felt so tired.

All of us were talking about the heat. We wanted to get fired up for an important game like this, but it's so hard in this weather. You end up worrying more about survival than victory. Pitchers hold back a little, pacing themselves. Batters swing at bad pitches, figuring the longer they wait to swing, the less strength they'll have.

One of our guys said it was all in the head, and another told the story about the manager who told his ballplayers one sweltering day that if he heard one man complaining about the heat, he'd fine the guy $100. About the fifth inning, the story goes, the starting pitcher walked to the dugout, wiped his forehead, and said, "Boy, is it hot out there!" He looked up, saw the manager glaring at him and, without missing a beat, added, "Just the way I like it!"

Mayo called me into his office before batting practice, and he and Wally Moses told me they'd like me to try a new stance—my fifth in five days. They told me I was crouching too low and that I'd never hit well that way. I thought I'd swung the bat pretty good last night, but they're the bosses. I said I'd lift up a little but all that changing around can really get you confused. After a while, you don't know which way is up.

After our batting practice, Mayo took forever to make out the starting lineup. He was in his office so long, making out lineups and ripping them up, that I yelled, "Hey, there's a palmist right down the street from our hotel."

I didn't yell too loud, just loud enough for my team-mates to hear, but not the manager.

Finally, one of the coaches came out of Mayo's office and told me I was playing first base today and Price was catching. Neither Kaline nor Cash were in the lineup. Al was so beat he never even came out and sat on the bench; he spent the entire game down in the cool tunnel leading from the clubhouse to the dugout.

We should've all stayed there.

We got a run in the first inning on Willie Horton's double—he had to come out of the game when he hurt himself sliding into second—and later Price hit a home run, and Denny McLain took a 4-2 lead into the fifth inning. He got one man out, then gave up a single to Frank Robinson. Mayo immediately brought in Daryl Patterson, and a couple of minutes later Ellie Hendricks hit a three-run home run and we were through. We were on our way to our third straight defeat, our second in Baltimore.

Some of the newspapermen were second-guessing Mayo afterward for taking Denny out so quickly. The writers didn't know that Denny had come to Mayo before the fifth inning and had said, "I'm losing it. Don't go too long with me." The writers didn't know because Mayo didn't volunteer the information, and Denny wasn't there. He'd left the park by the eighth inning.

We're thirteen and a half games behind the Orioles now. We're seven games over .500; they're thirty-four games over .500. All they have to do is win half of their remaining games, and they'll finish with ninety-eight victories.

We were awfully quiet in the clubhouse after the game. We're almost resigned to the fact that it's going to be impossible to catch the Orioles.

June 29

I didn't take batting practice today. With a double-header to play, I wanted to conserve my energy. While our guys hit, I sat in the dugout and talked to John Sain. "Don't let anybody get you confused," John said. "Some of our pitchers are confused. They're not getting much confidence from the manager, and I'm afraid the same thing's starting to happen to you. You've got eighty people whispering in your ear about how you should hit, what you should do. Well, forget it. Just go out there and do the thing the best way you know how. You've got to have confidence."

John has a way of making everything sound simple. He relaxed me and gave me a little faith in myself, in my ability. I hit the ball better today than I have in weeks.

Going into the ninth inning of the first game, we had only two hits off Mike Cuellar, Baltimore's top pitcher, and I had one of them. He hadn't walked anybody, and he had us shut out, 2-0.

But, suddenly, with two out in the ninth, Cuellar got wild. He walked two guys, and then Tresh got a hit, and it was 2-1, with Kaline coming up. The Orioles brought in Eddie Watt, a sidearm sinker-ball pitcher, to face Kaline. Watt's first pitch skipped by the catcher, a wild pitch that put our runners on second and third. Watt kind of kicked at the dirt a little, and we were up in the dugout now, screaming for Al, getting as excited as we'd been all series, probably all season. Al rapped the next pitch through the middle. Two runs raced in, and we were ahead, 3-2.

Lolich had been pitching for us, but we'd pinch-hit for him in the ninth. We had to go to the bullpen to hold the lead. Tom Timmerman came in, got a couple of guys out and then gave up a double. Chico Salmon came up to pinch-hit, and Mayo took Timmerman out and called in Mike Kilkenny. Mayo began telling Kilkenny how to pitch to Salmon, but Mike didn't let him get more than half a sentence out. "Don't worry, Skip," Mike said. "He's as good as out right now."

I just smiled and walked away. I told the umpire what Kilkenny had said. "Kilkenny's a rookie," I said. "I wouldn't have said something like that for the first five years I was in the league. Hell, the first five years, I said 'Sir' to the umpires."

The ump laughed. "The kids coming up now are cocky," I said. "Maybe that's why they seem to get better quicker."

And then, on the first pitch, Kilkenny got Salmon to pop up and end the ball game.

We'd finally beaten the Orioles—only the second time in seven meetings—and we'd done it with a finish right out of our 1968 pennant drive.

Mayo came back with Wilson in the second game. Earl had pitched only a couple of innings before getting knocked out Friday night, but he had a great lifetime record against the Orioles, so it was a good gamble.

The first Baltimore batter hit Wilson on the hand with a line drive, and Earl had to leave the game. Timmerman came in and, by the bottom of the second, Baltimore had a 3-1 lead. They had runners on first and second with two men out, and Mayo took out Timmerman and brought in Fred Lasher.

Lasher and Mayo haven't been getting along too well lately. Fred's been annoyed because he hasn't been working much, and he and the manager have had a few private meetings about it.

Now, as Fred was coming in from the bullpen, the Baltimore runner on second ducked into the dugout for a drink. Fred got to the mound and Mayo handed him the ball and said, "You know the situation now?"

Fred looked around. "Yeah," he said. "Man on first base."

"No," Mayo said.

Fred looked around again, "Man on first and man on third?" he said.

"No," Mayo said.

"Well, give me the goddamn ball," Fred said. "I don't care where they are. I'm going to get them out anyway."

Mayo walked off looking disgusted, but I can't blame Lasher. You can't see the game from the bullpen when you're warming up.

Lasher pitched to one batter and walked him, and Mayo wanted Lash out of the game. John Hiller wasn't sufficiently warmed up yet, so Mayo decided to stall. He walked slowly to the mound, and I walked out from behind the plate, and Cash walked over from first. The umps force you to make your moves right away if they think you're trying to stall, so we had to do some maneuvering. We had our backs to home plate, so the umpire couldn't catch our eyes and holler out to us to find out whether Mayo was just talking to the pitcher or was going to make a pitching change. I knew Mayo was going to change because he had come out to the mound and kicked the pitching rubber. If he's just going to talk to the pitcher, or make a suggestion, he doesn't kick the rubber. I don't know if Mayo knows he has this habit, but all the guys in the bullpen know it.

Mayo played it cool. "Now, don't turn around and look," he said, "but tell me when that home-plate umpire starts out here."

Norman and I began peeking out of the corners of our eyes.

"Hey, Norman," Mayo said. "Has he started yet?"

"Nope," Norman said.

We stood there, peeking.

"Now?" Mayo said.

"He's about halfway here," I said.

Just as the umpire got about three-quarters of the way out, Mayo signaled for Hiller.

Hiller was excellent. He gave up no runs, and I got a

two-run home run, my second hit of the game, and we were tied, 3-3, going into the eighth. Cash led off with a hit, Northrup struck out, and I came up. I tried to surprise them by bunting. I dropped a good one down the third-base line, but I'm not the fastest man in creation—and Brooks Robinson is the best third baseman in creation. I got nipped by half a step. Still, I'd moved Cash into scoring position. Matchick followed with a base hit, a line drive into center field, and as Cash came around third, Baltimore's Paul Blair dug up the ball and threw home. His throw was perfect. Cash was out by inches.

Hiller held them in the eighth, and we pinch-hit for him in the top of the ninth. We didn't score. In the bottom of the ninth, they got a runner to second base with two out. Don Buford was up, batting for the pitcher. Mayo came out to the mound. "Let's walk Buford," he told Don McMahon, "and pitch to Belanger."

"Mayo," I said, "if we do that, they're going to bring in Frank Robinson to bat for Belanger." Robinson hadn't played in the second game, and he was at the bat rack with his helmet on.

"Well, let's do what you want," Mayo said.

You hate to go against the manager, because it's his job that's on the line, but I said, "I'd rather pitch to Buford. Robby's the toughest out in the league. I'd rather have Buford beat me than him."

"Go ahead," Mayo said. "Pitch to Buford."

"Okay," I said. "I'll take the responsibility if you want to give it to me."

Mayo left, and I looked at McMahon. "Is this what you wanted to do?" I said.

"This is what I wanted to do," he said.

"Okay," I said. "Let's go get him."

I wasted a lot of hard thinking, because McMahon walked Buford anyway, though not intentionally. Robinson was announced as the pinch hitter, and Mayo made another pitching change. He brought in Dobson and told him, "Don't worry. If you get behind, I'll just bring in Kilkenny to face Powell."

As I was walking back to home plate, I was thinking about nobody but Robinson. The way Frank was hitting, I knew we were in some trouble. He could end this game just the way he'd ended so many others.

Robinson dug in. Dobson leaned in for my sign. All of a sudden, Norm Cash bolted across the infield, running faster than I'd ever seen him run. Some nut had thrown a cherry bomb on the field and it was smoldering on the ground next to first base. Norm sneaked back up and stepped on it, and luckily, the bomb didn't go off.

Robinson dug in again, and Pat got a quick strike on him. The next pitch, Frank lined a single into center field, exactly the kind of liner Matchick had hit an inning earlier with Cash on second. Mickey Stanley came up with the ball quickly, every bit as quickly as Blair had, and made a good throw to the plate, but by a fraction of a second, we missed getting the runner. We lost. We lost by a few inches.

Last year, those inches would have been ours.

June 30

Finally, after eighteen games in fifteen days, we had a day off today, and I relaxed. I played in a celebrity golf tournament honoring Gordie Howe, the great Detroit hockey player.

I'm only a fair golfer, a seven- or an eight-handicap when I'm playing regularly, a low-80s shooter, but today, after a few drinks, I went out and hit some balls farther than anyone could believe, just missed a hole-in-one, and shot a lovely 77.

When I'm playing baseball badly, I play golf great.

July 1

The Boston Red Sox arrived in Detroit today, in second place, eleven games behind Baltimore, two and a half games ahead of us.

We greeted them with twelve runs—more than we'd scored in all four games in Baltimore—and beat them easily. If we can sweep the three-game series, we'll be in second place.

We voted today for the All-Star team. You can't vote for anyone on your own team, and Mayo warned us that we shouldn't vote for our friends on the other teams, but for the best players. Mayo's going to be managing the American League All-Stars and he wants his strongest lineup. "Let's vote for all Baltimore players," someone shouted, "have Mayo play them for nine innings and hope somebody gets hurt."

July 2

Before tonight's game, Earl Wilson and Gates Brown walked up to Ike Brown and pounded him on the back. "Ike," Wilson said, "you've got a lot of weight on your shoulders today. You're the only soul brother in the lineup. We didn't have a brother out there last night, and they scored twelve runs. You've got to carry the colors for us today."

It was Earl who'd realized that during last night's game we used an all-white lineup, a real rarity these days in baseball—or any professional team sport, except hockey. I hadn't noticed it. "Last year," Mayo told me today, "when I'd take Horton out for defensive purposes during the World Series, I'd have an all-white lineup out there, and you should have seen the letters I got. I never even realized it."

Our integrated lineup did fine tonight. Tom Tresh went three-for-three, Don Wert hit a home run, Al Kaline made a super catch against the right-field screen and our stand-in first baseman made a fantastic bare-handed play on a ground ball. My hand started to swell up after that fantastic play, so I put ethyl chloride on it to freeze it, then went up to bat and hit a double.

Denny McLain pitched a 7-0 shutout, without even throwing hard, but he wasn't entirely happy. He lost twenty-five dollars, the fine for missing a signal to lay down a squeeze bunt. Denny can afford it.

After the game, I went into the Lindell A. C. with a couple of friends, and some guy came over and said, "Would you like to have a drink at my table?"

"I'm sorry," I said, "but I'm with some people."

"We're both from the University of Michigan," he said, "I sat next to you in class for three years. Can't you come over anyway?"

There were 25,000 students at the University of Michigan, and I didn't know this guy from Adam. But he had probably been telling his buddies what a great friend of his I'd been.

"I'm sorry," I said again. "But I'm with these people."

He said something under his breath. Then he called me a couple of obscene names and walked out.

I sat there steaming. I was glad the guy didn't come back or I might've gotten into trouble. I went up to the owner of the Lindell and told him that if that guy ever comes back into the place, they better get him out, because I'm afraid of what I might do to him.

It's absurd the way people think that an athlete, even when he's involved in his personal life, is public property. It's funny. When you're a kid you work so hard to become a star, and when you're there, so many of the trappings that go with it disturb you. One day last year, I took my kids to the monkey show at the zoo. We were sitting, waiting for the show to start, when some kids came over for autographs. I told them I'd sign, but only until the show started. When I said that, a couple of mothers became irate and said I was being a real donkey.

I do have an obligation. I know that. I think it's awfully important for kids to have a strong interest in something, whether it's academics or music or athletics. The kids you have to worry about aren't those who wear long hair, but the kids who can't get involved in anything. They just wander around and get into trouble. So if kids are interested in athletics and athletes, I'm going to help them all I can. I make speeches all the time urging communities not to cut back on funds for their physical education programs, and I go out of my way with pleasure to talk with kids and teach them things and, if it's all that important to them—although I've never been able to figure out why—to sign autographs.

But when adults start crowding in, often everything flies out of perspective. At dinner in Cleveland a while ago, a woman came over and asked Joe Sparma and me for our autographs. I said I'd be glad to sign as soon as we finished eating and, suddenly, as I was putting food in my mouth, she grabbed my arm, knocked the fork out of my hand, and said, "I've got to leave. Sign now."

Another time, at our golf club, a woman came over while I was having dinner with my wife, my parents, and some other relatives. I had a glass of champagne in my hand, and she grabbed hold of me from the back, spilling the champagne all over the place, and planted a big, wet kiss on me. After that, what had been a nice, quiet family dinner turned into a circus, with people coming up from all over the place to intrude and ask for autographs.

If someone doesn't have common decency, then I won't sign an autograph. Even as a kid, I never did understand why people wanted autographs, anyway. If I got to meet a guy and shake hands and say hello, well, that was beautiful. I met Gordie Howe once, when I was ten, and he was real nice and he said, "It's nice to meet you and good luck." What was important, what thrilled me, was the impression the man made on me. I didn't need an autograph. I didn't have to show other people proof that I'd met him.

July 3

We won our third in a row from Boston today and moved into second place. We're back to ten games over .500, and we've moved to within eleven games of the Orioles, who've lost two in a row, a disaster by their standards.

Beginning tomorrow, we have a four-game series with Baltimore here in Detroit. If we can sweep that series, we'll be back in contention. We'll definitely have the Orioles looking over their shoulders.

They were looking over my shoulder today. They had an off-day, so they came into Detroit and three of them —Dave McNally, Mark Belanger, and Dave Johnson— sat in the front row behind home plate, offering me free advice. A few times, I turned around and asked them what pitch to call, and they said something unprintable. When I hit a home run, my second this series, they gave me a little ovation. It was all very friendly. It won't be tomorrow.

I'm starting to feel better, starting to feel like I can get a decent season going and we can move up in the pennant race. Other people, too, are beginning to suspect the Tigers may not be finished. I've got a clipping pasted in my locker from the *Detroit Free Press,* and next to a cartoon showing a dead tiger with his tombstone inscribed, "R.I.P., June 22, 1969," there's an article that begins, "The end came today. . . ."

The author of that article came up to me today and said, "Now that you're beginning to win, I'm going to have to talk with you and get back in your good graces."

"You've already written us off," I said. "Why bother even coming to the games?"

"You never know what's going to happen," he said.

"You should've thought of that on June 22," I said.

I felt almost as cocky as I sounded.

Two Tigers went to the dentist today. Mickey Stanley hadn't been able to eat for two days, and he had to have a couple of teeth pulled. He arranged to have the dental work done at 7 A.M., so that he could make the game. Denny McLain had to have caps put on his teeth. We never saw him all day.

July 4

After four innings of the first game of the scheduled doubleheader with Baltimore today, we were beating the Orioles, 4-1. But rain was coming down, and a ball game has to last at least four and a half innings before the result can be official. We prayed for the rain to stop, but with the Orioles' luck this year, I expected, at the minimum, a hurricane.

In the top of the fifth, Mickey Lolich started to rush. He threw seven straight balls, and I remembered a game last year when the White Sox were leading us in the rain and needed only three more outs to make the game official. Their pitcher, Gary Peters, hurried, lost his rhythm, gave up a couple of walks, then a couple of hits, then a grand-slam home run by Earl Wilson. We scored six runs and won the game.

I trotted out to the mound. "Just forget about the rain," I told Mickey. "Pitch like you regularly would. Forget about trying to speed up on account of the rain."

Mickey settled down and got the Orioles out in the top of the fifth, and the game was official. But the umpires weren't ready to call the game off. They had the ground crew cover the infield with the tarp. Both clubs retreated to their dugouts to wait and see if the rain would stop.

Now, we wanted the rain to go on forever. We wanted that victory. Most of the players went into the locker room to listen to music, but I stayed in the dugout. I don't like to let my body temperature change during a game. I sat with Tom Tresh, three other players, and the umpires, and I looked at Hank Soar, the chief umpire, then poked Tresh and said, "Well, I've lived in Detroit almost thirty years and this looks like one of those all-day rains."

Tom picked right up. "Yeah, sure looks like it," he said.

Soar didn't react, so we called down to the locker room for Daryl Patterson, who is part Indian, and Daryl came out and did a rain dance. Still, Soar didn't react, so Cash sneaked up behind one of the other umps, Emmett Ashford, who was standing with his hands in his back pockets. Norman slipped his own arms around Ashford and signaled to the TV cameras that the game was over. From a distance, it looked as if Emmett were giving the sign. Emmett didn't think Cash was too funny. Sometimes the umpires just don't have a sense of humor.

While we were waiting, we talked on the bench about how other people in this world were spending their time on the Fourth of July—at picnics, on the beaches, watching fireworks—every way except staring at puddles and hoping to play baseball. We sat for a long time, kidding around and needling and complaining.

We were also talking about Earl Weaver, the Oriole manager, and how he might react to a defeat in the minimum number of innings necessary to make a game official. Weaver's a fiery little guy, and a lot of us are figuring—praying, really—that he may be our secret weapon for winning the pennant. He's a rookie manager who hasn't been through a major-league season, and some guys have told me that in the minor leagues, when things went wrong, he was a tough guy for his players to get along with. I'd heard that he used to sit on the team's valuables box after a bad game and defy anyone to come and get his wallet; he wanted his players to just sit and think about what they'd been doing wrong. We're wondering what might happen if the Orioles went into a tailspin and Weaver pulled a minor-league trick like that on Frank Robinson, who's pretty tough himself. We'd like to see what'd happen then.

Finally, at 5:30, the umpires called the game. We moved within ten games of the Orioles. I went into the trainer's room, and a bunch of guys were sitting there, drinking beer. "Hey," one of them said. "I sure hope this rain didn't spoil anybody's picnic."

July 5

We got beat, 16-0, today, and we laughed all through the game. It was the annual Father-Son game, and after we clowned with the kids, then we had to get tough— shift gears entirely—and face the Baltimore Orioles.

We had a chance to go twelve games over .500 for the first time all season, but we didn't make it. We tried. We tried hard. Mayo played a few hunches, a few gambles. He put Kaline at first base, Tracewski at shortstop, Tresh in the outfield, then brought Pat Dobson in from the bullpen to start the game.

Mayo's hunches backfired. In the first inning, Tracewski made an error at shortstop, Tresh made an error in the outfield, and Dobson allowed four runs. We completely violated Freehan's Law: never beat yourself. That was also John McGraw's Law when he managed the New York Gaints, Abner Doubleday's when he invented the game, and, I guess, the Marquis de Sade's.

Still, in the fifth inning, we were trailing by only two runs, 4-2, when Paul Blair led off for Baltimore with a triple. Frank Robinson came up, swung at a pitch and missed, and his bat flew out of his hand and skidded past the third baseman. I had the ball in my hand and nobody had called time out, so as the third-base coach retrieved that bat, and Blair was "cool walking" slowly back to third base, I thought, "Look at that man just standing there. I wonder what would happen if I trotted down and tagged him."

I started up the third base line real slow. About halfway there, I said to myself, "Let's try it." I took off full speed and the people in the stands helped me by not screaming to warn Blair. I shot up behind Blair and tagged him out. Earl Weaver went wild. But there was nothing he could do. When I got back to the plate, I told Frank Robinson, "We've been practicing that one since spring training."

Robinson struck out, but then Boog Powell singled, so the play on Blair saved us a run. But it wasn't enough to save the game. They scored five runs in the eighth inning and whipped us, 9-3. Dave McNally was the winning pitcher, the third time he's beaten us this season. He's not an overpowering pitcher, but he works that strike zone. You always come back saying, "I'm not afraid to hit against him, but he gets me out so easy." He was a little wild at the start today, but he got himself together and held on until they broke the game open. When your club is hot, you can hang in there like that.

July 6

Before the game today, our guys were kidding Paul Blair about getting picked off third base yesterday. "How could a 215-pound guy tiptoe up behind a jackrabbit like you?" someone said.

Blair laughed. "When Freehan touched me," he said, "I thought some fan had run out of the stands. It wasn't so bad getting picked off, but if it had to happen, I wish I'd been the third out of the inning. Then I wouldn't have had to go back to the dugout and face Weaver."

We weren't in too much of a laughing mood today. The *Detroit News* buried us again. We won four in a row—three from Boston, one from Baltimore—then lost one, and the paper wrote us off. We kept boosting each other up, telling each other that we still had a chance.

Al Kaline hit a home run to get us off to a 1-0 lead, then Baltimore went ahead, 3-1, on Boog Powell's home run over the right-field roof. Only four men had ever done that before—Ted Williams, Mickey Mantle, Norm Cash, and Don Mincher—but Powell can hit the ball to Mars. The next time Boog came up, I trotted out to McLain and said, "What have you got in mind?"

"The best thing I can do," Denny said, "is give the sign of the cross before I throw the ball."

We loaded the bases in the fourth inning with none out, and I hit into a double play. I can't hit with men on base to save my soul. I don't know what's wrong, but it's got to be psychological. I've been hitting my few home runs with nobody on base.

We tied up the score, anyway, and in the sixth inning, McAuliffe hit a home run, and Tresh came up. I was sitting on the bench next to Stanley, and we began talking about Tom's slump. He'd been the hottest batter on the team for a while, after some lessons from Wally Moses, but suddenly he'd gotten all messed up again. Mickey and I are two other prize students of Wally's, so now, as Tresh came up, Mickey said, "You know, Wally's got Tommy all screwed up. There's no way he can hit." Just as Mickey said that, Tom hit the ball into the upper deck, putting us ahead, 5-3.

Hendricks got a home run for them in the eighth. With the score 5-4, two out in the ninth, and Paul Blair on base, Frank Robinson came up. Denny didn't have his good stuff, but he'd been battling hard, keeping the Orioles off-balance, fighting out of jams. He got two quick strikes on Frank, then threw two balls. I figured Frank would be looking for a breaking ball and Denny agreed with me.

So Denny threw a sidearm fast ball low and away. The umpire called strike three, Denny had his thirteenth victory of the season, and we were eleven games over .500, ten games out of first place.

Later, Robinson told some reporters he didn't think the pitch was high enough to be a strike. "The umpires," Frank was quoted as saying, "were more up-tight about this series than the players."

Maybe the Orioles are getting a little shook up. Maybe Earl Weaver's going to have to start sitting on the valuables box.

July 7

We're in Boston, where they play lots of day games and lots of kids always line the path from the bus to the locker room, pleading for autographs. The kids all talk with the "pahk-the-cahr" accent. They'll grab hold of you as you're walking to the locker room and say, "How about an autograph, mistah?" If you disappoint one of them by saying "I can't sign now; wait'll later," he'll usually look at you real hard—even the little ones do this—and say, "Why you deerty bahstahrd!"

One of the Boston writers, Cliff Keene, is always needling us. Last week, in Detroit, he was on Tresh. The first game there against the Red Sox, Tommy hit a couple of home runs, so Keene came to the locker room before the second game and told Tresh, "We've got a kid pitching today you won't be able to hit."

"There isn't anyone I can't hit," Tom said.

"He's going to throw you nothing but curves," Keene said.

"That doesn't matter."

"Well," Keene said, "if you hit a curve ball for a home run today, I'll kiss your tail right here in the clubhouse in front of everybody."

"I'll take you up on that," Tom said.

Tom got a double and a home run off curve balls in the game, but Keene never showed up in the locker room.

Today, as we were getting dressed for the game, we saw Keene peeking through the little glass window in the door of the clubhouse. Tresh was just about in the middle of getting dressed, and someone yelled, "Hold it, Tommy. Here comes your boy. If he wants to get in here, he's going to have to keep his promise."

We all began hollering at Keene. "If you want to come in here," somebody said, "you better be prepared to back up your promise." We were ready for him; we even had the spot marked.

Keene disappeared. He never even came on the field.

Right before the game, I went up to our trainer and said, "Got any desire pills?" He laughed, but I wish there were something like that. Sometimes I'll be sitting on the bench in one of those listless moods that come on any ballplayer and I'll tell somebody to slap me hard on the face. Just to wake me up, to generate some enthusiasm.

We were all listless, and we were beaten, 7-2. Their pitcher, Ray Culp, knocked Donny Wert down once, and I said to Kaline, "I wish somebody would do that to me to get some of my adrenaline going." I sure need something to get me stirred up.

July 8

I ran into Mayo at the hotel this afternoon, and he said, "Congratulations."

"For what?" I said.

"You were selected for the All-Star team," he said.

"Thanks," I said. "There goes a three-day vacation."

Mayo laughed. "We've all got to be there," he said.

"Well, I hope you don't catch me fifteen innings." In 1967, the All-Star Game went fifteen innings and I caught them all.

"Don't worry," Mayo said.

Actually, my wife and I, and my stockbroker, Jerry LeVan, and his wife had already made plans with some friends in Washington for us all to get together during the All-Star Game there. I was just agitating Mayo a little.

Later in the day, in the seventh inning out at Fenway Park, a foul ball banged into the knuckle of my right hand. It really cracked. I thought for sure I'd broken a bone, and Mayo and the trainer both came running out. "Get in there and get some ice on it," Mayo said, "and we'll get an ambulance to take you to the hospital for X rays."

Meanwhile, the trainer was spraying the hand with ethyl chloride, and when he finished, I said, "Mayo, I think it's going to be all right."

"That's all right," Mayo said. "We'll get Price in there."

"Well, if you want to get Price in there," I said, "that's fine. But my hand is all right."

He left me in, but after the game, he said, "Now, are you sure it's all right?"

"Yeah," I said. "It didn't bother me throwing. I've got all the movement you could expect. It'll be a little sore to-morrow. That's all."

I don't know what's going through Mayo's mind, but it sort of scares me to think that maybe he wants me to get hurt so he can play Price. The past couple of years I've led the team in games played. I want to do that again. I don't want to sit on the sidelines.

The club was listless again tonight, and we lost again. You run into streaks like that. But last year we played a lot of games where we'd be listless early on, and we always seemed to spark ourselves in the last three innings. This year we just don't have that belief in ourselves; we can't quite come up with that last blind charge in which you win the game or, at least, scare the hell out of somebody. We're down to only nine games over .500, and the situation looks almost hopeless again.

July 9

With a day game following a night game, Mayo decided to rest Kaline and announced that Gates Brown would start today. In batting practice, Gates pulled a muscle. Since Gates does his best as a pinch hitter, never as a starter, we told him that his muscle popped the minute he saw his name in the lineup. "Good old Gates," somebody jokingly said. "Bench me or trade me, but don't play me regularly." Gates really was hurt.

We beat the Red Sox, 6-5, a real struggle.

The afternoon paper printed the results of the All-Star voting, and I was the only Tiger in the starting lineup. In fact, I was the only Tiger who even came close. Cash, our hottest hitter, got only one vote at first base; Kaline had only seventeen votes in the outfield; and McAuliffe, who I thought had a good chance, didn't even come in second in the voting at second base.

The guys congratulated me—in their fashion. "Nice going," Northrup said. "By the way, can I use your cottage for three days?"

"Thanks a lot," I said. "You really know how to hurt a guy."

"I'll never be selected for the All-Star Game," Northrup said. "I don't even know if I want to be selected. One of the things I live for in this game is the three-day All-Star break. It lets me get myself back together physically and mentally."

I came into the league in 1963, and since my second season, I haven't had an All-Star break. I'd like to have those three days to get myself back together, but, of course, I take a lot of pride in being picked for the game. I'm not too proud this year. There's only one other catcher in the whole league who's playing regularly. I'm the All-Star catcher almost by default.

July 10

We started a five-game series with Cleveland in Detroit tonight—we play the last-place Indians nine times in the next eleven days leading up to the All-Star break—and we didn't get off to a good start.

I played first base and, in the seventh inning, when they got four runs to move ahead of us, 5-2, I watched three balls go past me, all base hits, all just beyond my reach. A good first baseman might've reached all three.

The fans booed me—probably some of the same fans who last year greeted me, after the World Series, by decorating my house and painting Freehan Drive on my street —and, for a while, I thought McLain might join them. Denny, who didn't finish the game, wasn't too happy with my fielding.

We lost in extra innings, and afterward, in the clubhouse, I walked up to McLain. "I'm trying to do the best job I can," I said. "I'm not out there for defensive purposes. Don't be blaming your troubles on anybody but yourself."

Denny mumbled something about my being out of position. "Well, you can be the director from now on," I said. "When you're not pitching, you sit on the bench and watch me and when you think I ought to move, you just direct me to the spot. You ought to do a good job. You know just where I ought to be. There's only one problem: You don't usually stay on the bench very long."

"Don't worry," Denny said. "I'll be out there."

That's my pitcher.

I'm his catcher.

We sure get along great, don't we?

July 11

At nine o'clock this morning, Ernie Harwell, the Tigers' broadcaster, picked me up at my house and drove me up to Saginaw, Michigan, to sign autographs at the Saginaw Savings and Loan Bank. Ernie does commercials for the bank and two months ago, when I was feeling a little stronger, I'd agreed to make this appearance with him. "A quick one," he said. "Just sign a couple of autographs and come on back."

There must've been five thousand kids at the bank, and it was a madhouse. Kids were trampling each other, and we ended up signing autographs for more than two hours, one right after another. Then we went to a country club for a steak, and by the time I got home, it was four o'clock. I made a few phone calls, had a glass of iced tea with my wife and daughters, then took off for the ball park. I don't know if I was really ready to play.

I was at first base again, and in the third inning, I made an error on a routine grounder that started off a big Cleveland rally. The Indians beat us, 8-1; our only run was a home run by Jim Price. I felt extra bad because I made the error behind my roomie, Joe Sparma, and I didn't get any hits. I was no help at all.

A muscle in my chest—one that's used in throwing—has been bothering me. Whenever I took a breath tonight, it killed me; I couldn't even talk loud because any little exertion hurt. I told the trainer I wanted to see a doctor after the game. The doctor checked me out and said there was nothing wrong with my heart and lungs, that the trouble had to be muscular. He said I'd probably torn the muscles between the ribs. He gave me some anti-inflammation pills and told me to pack ice on the ribs all night. "When you tear muscles in your ribs," he said, "they take a long time to heal." He scared the hell out of me.

July 12

I soaked my ribs in ice all last night and was feeling better this morning. Then I got to the park and sneezed and tore everything to shreds again. The team doctor looked at me and had the trainer give me sound and ice treatments. Then I went to see Mayo, and he asked if I could hit. "Yeah, I can probably hit," I said, "but the thing is never going to get better if I keep irritating it." So I didn't play.

I sure was missed. We had eleven runs by the end of the second inning and beat the Indians, 15-3. Price had another home run and five runs batted in. That's more RBIs than I get in a month.

The spirit on our club these days leaves something to be desired. A lot of guys have been ducking into the clubhouse after coming out of a game, instead of sitting on the bench and rooting. I can understand if the guy's a pitcher, if he's got to go in for a shower and an arm rub after pitching, but the other guys don't have any good excuse. Worse, some of the guys have been staying in the clubhouse, instead of coming out to the bench, even before they've played in the game. The other night, Mayo wanted to use Willie Horton as a pinch hitter and looked around and couldn't find him. Willie, who's been hurt for a couple of weeks now, was in the locker room; fortunately, he was in uniform. Ike Brown ran and got him, and Willie pinch-hit.

But today we had a full team on the bench, for a change; even Denny was there. The reason was that Mayo ordered John Hand, our clubhouse man, to lock the clubhouse at 1:15 P.M., fifteen minutes before game time, and not open it "until I say so."

Once we got our big lead, some of the guys started clowning on the bench, raising their hands when Mayo's back was turned and asking permission to go to the bathroom. Denny brought two boxes of candy bars and some ice-cream bars to the dugout and spread them out so that the guys who couldn't get into the clubhouse could still have their regular rations. Mayo may not be treating us exactly like men by locking the door, but we're not acting like men either.

On the other hand, though, we've got a guy like Dick McAuliffe who's playing with torn cartilage in his knee. Dick told me that he can't move his knee when he gets up in the morning, that his wife has to help him out of bed. But he hasn't told the manager. He doesn't want Mayo to know how much pain he's in. He wants to play. I wish we all did.

July 13

Jimmy Price has been so hot lately the writers have begun calling him "Slugger," "Killer," "Babe Ruth," names like that, and the guys kid me that I'll end up like Wally Pipp, the Yankee first baseman who once took a day off, was replaced by a kid named Lou Gehrig, and never got back in the lineup again.

I'm glad to see Jimmy doing well. I don't want him to take my job away, but I root like hell for him and I help him any way I can. There's no antagonism between us; any time I'm upset because he's in the lineup instead of me, I'm angry with myself or with the manager or with some injury or something. But never with Jimmy.

Before the Cleveland doubleheader today, Mayo asked me to take a little batting practice to see if I could hit. The first two balls I hit sailed out of the park. "Looks like it doesn't hurt you to swing," he said.

"It's all right when I swing," I said, "but it isn't when I throw."

I could have lied and persuaded Mayo to let me play today, but I know I would've set back the healing process.

Before the first game, some guy in the stands started yelling at me, "What kind of All-Star are you? You can't even play ahead of Price." My pride hurt worse than my ribs.

Jimmy drove in three runs with a hit with the bases loaded, and we won the first game. It's not so bad to play behind a guy who can do something like that.

The satisfaction of winning the first game didn't last very long. The Indians came back and whipped us in the second game.

Dick McAuliffe didn't start either game. Mayo knows now how badly the torn cartilage has been bothering him. Mac probably needs an operation, but the club wants him to wait till the All-Star break to see how serious the problem is. Mayo did use him as a pinch hitter in the second game today, and as Mac was being announced, the manager called down to the bullpen and said, "Send up the Ohio State quarterback to run for McAuliffe if he gets on."

The Ohio State quarterback is my roomie, Joe Sparma, former first-string signal caller for Woody Hayes. Joe hurried up to the bench, but he didn't have to run for McAuliffe. Bad leg and all, Dick hit a home run.

"Why didn't you trot it out for Dick?" Hal Naragon, our bullpen coach, asked Sparma after the game.

"Mayo wouldn't let me," Sparma said. "He was afraid I wouldn't know which way to run. And he was sure that even if he pointed me in the right direction, I'd screw up and miss first base."

July 14

At the airport today, getting ready to fly from Detroit to Washington, we got word that Denny wasn't going to be on the flight. Mayo had received a call from Denny's doctor and had been told that Denny was in the hospital with an arm inflammation. When the guys heard this, some of them wanted to bet that Denny was in his own plane, on his way to Florida.

Denny was supposed to open the Washington series tonight, and Mayo wasn't certain who would take his place. At 3:30, four and a half hours before the game, I was in the locker room, getting sound treatments for my arm. The phone rang, and I answered. Ted Williams was calling to find out who was pitching for us. "Damned if I know," I said.

Right before the game, Mayo handed the ball to Sparma. "Do the best you can," Mayo said.

Joe laughed. "Hell," he said, "the farther down on the list I get, the more I pitch. I'll have more starts than the guys in the regular rotation. Mayo, you just can't keep me hidden."

Mayo had to laugh, too.

Joe didn't have his control. I think he walked six men in the first three innings. It was a good time, I guess, for me to be out in the bullpen, nursing my injury. Cash told Sparma during the game that Price looked like a flagman on an aircraft carrier the way he was jumping around trying to catch Joe's pitches.

Joe Coleman pitched for Washington and shut us out, 3-0. Last year, Coleman had the best record in the league against us—four victories, no defeats. He just walks to the mound and beats us.

July 15

President Nixon came to the game today and proved he's a baseball fan by staying through the whole nine innings. I got back into the lineup, the first time I'd ever played in front of a President. I made no errors at first base and got one hit, so I'm now fielding 1.000 and batting .333 in front of Presidents. I'm really great under pressure.

Al Kaline was batting in front of me today, and I could see from the on-deck circle how closely the President was watching him. Al campaigned for President Nixon last year, and he's a member of the advisory staff of the President's Council on Physical Fitness. Al tried to put on a good show for his man today, but he hit into a couple of double plays and never hit the ball hard.

I had my politician there, too, the man I'd supported for President in 1968—Senator Eugene McCarthy. We'd met when he was covering the World Series for *Life* Magazine last year, and we'd chatted then about sports and the war in Vietnam. I respected him and I was glad to see him again, but I couldn't help thinking that I was for him in 1968, and he's for me in 1969, and neither one of us has been too good for the other.

We lost. We came up with a triple play—afterward, the guys were telling John Sain, "You ought to teach that triple play pitch to all your men"—but we lost, 7-3.

We're at the bottom now. We're in third place. We've lost seven out of ten games and we're 47-40, only seven games over .500. We're fourteen and a half games behind Baltimore, the greatest gap of the season. Our chances aren't too bright.

Afterward, in the locker room, Norm Cash looked at me and said, "I'm sure glad I've got a good-paying job in the off-season."

"Have you got any openings?" I said. "I might need a job myself."

July 16

Mayo called one of his rare meetings tonight. "Gentlemen," he said, before the game, "you were world champions last year and the Senators came in last. The last two nights they've beaten you, and they've done it playing great baseball. It looks like they're expecting things to go their way. They're doing things as a team; they're battling and they're fighting. We're not. We're thinking too much of ourselves as individuals. We're not trying to move runners along the bases. We're more concerned with trying for that hit, more concerned with individual statistics— whether I got three-for-three tonight—than with team statistics. The Senators are improved because they're playing as a team. That's why they're only two games behind us right now. We're better than that. We've got more ability than we've shown so far."

Mayo jammed both hands in his back pockets. "Gentlemen," he said, "a lot of funny things can happen in this game. We had better start doing things right or else something is going to happen. I don't want to make this sound like a pep talk, but if you can't play, if you're not 100 percent, if you're tired or something, you come in and tell me because I want to get a guy in that lineup who can give 100 percent. Those are the guys I want on that field. To win, it takes twenty-five guys like that. I don't know why you're playing like this, why you're doing things like this. Maybe it's lack of concentration. But let's go out there and start doing things right from here on in."

That was the meeting. The guys moved out, and Mayo called me into his office. He wanted to know if I could catch today. "I don't know," I said. "I haven't had a chance to test my arm, at least not from the catcher's position. I know I'm not 100 percent—like you said in that meeting. Let's leave it this way. I'll go out and try to extend my arm and if it's all right, then you can play me."

"I don't want to do that," he said.

"Well," I said, "if you've got to be 100 percent to play this game, then I'm in trouble. I'm only 100 percent about fifty games a year. I need to play more than that to keep in shape."

Mayo laughed. "Well, I wasn't that serious," he said, "but I just want you to let me know if it bothers you." A little later, when I told him I'd be able to play, he told me to forget it, to spend the game out in the bullpen.

Lolich pitched and won the game. He's 13-2 now and leading the league in strikeouts.

Even though we beat the Senators tonight, they put up a good struggle. I'm impressed by them. All the money Ted Williams is getting to manage Washington, he's earning. Already, the Senators' attendance is higher than it was all last season. The town is suddenly interested in the baseball team. This is a racially troubled town and if the black community has baseball on its mind through the summer—at least a little bit—then it's just that much less apt to blow up.

Last year, after two summers with riots, Detroit was fairly quiet. People said that interest in our pennant race helped a great deal. Lots of people were talking about baseball, listening to the games, and watching the games, and that helped take their minds off their problems. That's hardly a sociological solution; that hardly gets inside the wound. But it's a Band-Aid. It doesn't hurt. Instead of President Nixon introducing riot-control bills, maybe he ought to figure out how there could be twenty-four pennants in twenty-four cities.

July 17

The Washington fans are really excited about their team. We were leading them, 4-3, in the bottom of the eighth inning tonight, they had two men on base, and the crowd was screaming as if it were the World Series—not a third-place team against a fourth-place team.

I was catching, for the first time in a week, and Fred Lasher was pitching for us. The more the crowd yelled, the harder Lash threw. I walked out to the mound to calm him down. "Hi, Fred," I said. "Ever play in a one-run game before? Just relax. Don't try to throw the ball through the wall behind me. Keep your cool. Relax."

Fred got out of the inning. Then, in the bottom of the ninth, with the score still 4-3 and one man out, Lash gave up a triple to Del Unser. The crowd went out of its mind. Tim Cullen was up. Frank Howard was on deck.

You have to be cool in a situation like that. "I'm as square as an ice cube and twice as cool," Gates Brown used to say when he was getting all those crucial pinch hits for us last year.

Lasher wasn't cool. He walked Unser, and Mayo Smith

came out to the mound. "Gimme the ball, Lasher," he said. He was teed off.

"I want to pitch to Howard," Lasher said. "It isn't my fault they got those runs."

"Just give me the goddamn ball," Mayo said. "You walked that guy on first. Don't blame me. Now shut up and get out of here."

Don McMahon came in. "What do you want to do?" I said.

"I'm going with my best pitch, my fast ball, and try and strike him out," McMahon said.

"Your breaking ball is really improved," I said. "Let's go with that and get a double play." Actually, Don hasn't been throwing that good a curve, but I wanted him to try one on Howard. A fast ball is always a risk to Frank and, with a curve, there's a better chance to get him to hit the ball on the ground. Howard doesn't run that well, and we've got a good chance for the double play, I figure, if he hits it on the ground.

McMahon's first pitch was a hanging curve, and Howard topped it to the shortstop. We got the double play, winning the game, and inside, Mayo immediately called Lasher to his office. They had some words, and the guys began agitating Lasher when he came out, calling him "Leaky Lips" for talking back to the manager. I can't get upset with Fred for getting angry at the manager over being taken out of a game. But I do think Fred should have more control over his emotions when he's pitching. A relief pitcher can't be nervous.

July 18

Denny McLain called my hotel room in Cleveland this afternoon and said, "What time is the game?"

"It's 7:45," Sparma said.

"Well," Denny said. "I guess I'll make it."

Denny, who was scheduled to be the starting pitcher,

was calling from Detroit. And Denny, who is going to revolutionize this game, had decided to fly to Cleveland in his own plane. He had trouble with one of his engines in mid-flight, had to head back to Detroit to change planes, and finally got to the park at 7:10. Cash came in after infield practice, saw Denny getting dressed, and took him by the hand and walked him into Mayo's office. "This is a guy named Dennis McLain," Norman said. "He'd like to pitch tonight."

A few other guys admitted they were honored that McLain had finally joined us on the road trip. "During the winter," Northrup said, "they ought to take McLain into the hospital and make sure his liver, his teeth, his arm, his back, everything, is all right, so he doesn't have any excuses next year."

Denny went out and pitched, and after the first inning I told Kaline, "Denny's got nothing tonight. But, you watch, he'll pitch a shutout."

They hit line drives off him all night. Willie Horton ran all over the field and tied a record for most putouts by an outfielder. But we got four runs—I hit a home run, and so did Horton—and Cleveland got none. "What did I tell you?" I said to Kaline in the clubhouse. "He's unbelievable. He had nothing. He just finessed them all night long, kept the ball down, and we won."

July 19

My wife came to the game today. Pat flew to Cleveland so that we can leave together for the All-Star Game. We're going to spend Monday at a 2,000-acre farm in Roanoke, Virginia, then go into Washington Tuesday.

Usually, I don't take my wife on the road. She's a jinx. A couple of years ago, she went on a road trip with me, and we didn't win a single game, so last year she didn't travel at all. But this year she said flatly that she doesn't believe in that jinx stuff. And she certainly wasn't a jinx today.

We beat Cleveland again, our fourth straight victory, and I had two hits and four RBIs, my biggest game since the second game of the season.

I was proud of something else, too. I was up once with a runner on second and nobody out and, after failing twice to bunt the man over to third, I didn't go for the big hit with two strikes and the bunt sign off. Instead, I just punched a little grounder to the right side of the infield and got the runner to third that way. Northrup came in to pinch-hit and drove in the run with a sacrifice fly. That's what Mayo was talking about the other day—doing things for the team. The value of those ground balls doesn't show up in the batting average, but I hope the manager and general manager remember when they make up the contracts.

July 20

It was raining so hard when we woke up today that I told my wife we wouldn't be able to walk across the street for nine o'clock mass. "There's no way they can get this doubleheader in," I said. But then I looked at the schedule and saw we'd be coming to Cleveland only once more all season—for games on September 10 and September 11. A rain-out would mean we'd have to play two doubleheaders in a row in September, and that would be awfully tough. So I knew they'd make every effort to get these games in.

Because of the rain, we didn't take any batting practice. At 12:15, Mayo called a meeting. He looked around and said, "Are all my athletes here?" The answer was no. It was forty-five minutes before the game was due to start, and our rule is that players have to be in the locker room at least two hours before game time on the road and three hours at home. But Jim Price was missing, and so was our ace right-hander. They'd flown to Detroit to spend Saturday night with their families, and because of the bad weather, Denny was having trouble getting his plane back into Cleveland.

As Mayo took his head count, the phone rang. It was the American League president, Joe Cronin, calling to tell Mayo that Dave Johnson, Baltimore's second baseman, wouldn't be able to play in the All-Star Game and that Mike Andrews of Boston would have to be called in to replace him. Cronin also wanted to know if Denny McLain were going to be the starting pitcher in the All-Star Game.

"Denny?" Mayo said. "Well, ah, he's not around."

"What do you mean?" Cronin said. "It's forty-five minutes before game time."

"Well, he's up flying around someplace," Mayo said.

The guys broke up. Obviously, the president of the American League doesn't know Denny the way we do.

While Denny and Price were up in the air, Mayo held his meeting. "I'm happy the way you've been playing team baseball, like hitting behind the runners," he said. "This type of thing is responsible for the way we've been winning lately."

And then Mayo gave the guys a reward. With the All-Star Game scheduled for Tuesday, we'd normally be back for practice on Wednesday, but Mayo said, "There will be no practice on Wednesday. But I don't want to see you coming in here on Thursday with sunburns. Anybody who comes back with a sunburn gets a $200 fine."

"Me, too, Skip?" said Gates Brown.

The guys applauded Mayo's speech. All the players not in the All-Star Game—which means everybody but McLain, Lolich, and me—are going to spend the three days with their families as the guests of a resort hotel outside Detroit.

McLain and Price showed up shortly after the meeting. Price dressed in a hurry and went out to catch. I played first base, and we got in two innings before the rain sent us back to the locker room and the dugouts for a long wait.

During the break, I saw something I'd never seen before: Hawk Harrelson climbed out of the Cleveland dugout, went into the stands, sat down, and began signing autographs. There's a league rule against that, and a fine for breaking the rule. The umpires were in our dugout, and when Nestor Chylak saw Harrelson, all he could say was "Holy mackerel!"

Chylak picked up our dugout phone and dialed the home-team dugout to talk to the Cleveland manager, Alvin Dark. "I hope that you know your star is up in the stands signing autographs for the people," Chylak said.

"Yeah, I know," Dark said. "Fine him if you want to. But Harrelson said he wanted to do it, and we have a tough enough time drawing people in this city, so let him do it."

The Hawk signed for fifteen minutes and later, after the game got underway again, the people gave him a big ovation every time he came to bat. Dark told me later that Harrelson is the best public-relations man in baseball. Probably, he is. He grabs every bit of press he can, so he can make as much money from this game as he can. He's got the right idea. He's the best paid .240 hitter in baseball.

Lolich started, but he needed help. Lasher relieved him in the seventh, then McMahon came in for Lash in the ninth. At about 4:15—just as the Apollo 11 astronauts were about to land on the moon—we were ahead, 3-2, with two outs and two Indians on base. Harrelson walked to load the bases and everybody was nervous— especially McMahon. As Harrelson trotted to first, I said to him, "Right now, two men are trying to land on the moon, and McMahon is more nervous over his situation than those astronauts are over theirs. Hell, just think how insignificant this game is in comparison to what they're doing."

"Yeah," the Hawk said. "I've got to admit my butt would be a little tighter if I was in their situation."

Then McMahon struck out Tony Horton to end the game. We had won five straight games. We were twelve games over .500 for the first time all year.

Late in the second game, with the score tied, Tony Horton came to bat. He'd already hit a home run and a single. "You didn't do so well in the first game," I said, "but I was playing first base then. Now I'm catching and you hit a home run. As long as I'm back here calling the signals, you'll never look bad."

Tony laughed, then said, "Are you done talking now?"

"Why?" I said. "Does that bother you?"

"Yeah," he said.

As I'd been talking, I'd put down my signal, and I hadn't been paying much attention to what I was calling. Just as Daryl Patterson was in the middle of winding up, I realized that I didn't know what I'd called. So I yelled out, "I don't know what I called here—be alive!"

It was a fast ball, right down the middle, and Horton took it for a strike. Then he jumped out of the batter's box and began complaining to the umpire about my talking. He said he wanted that pitch over again. Was he mad! He finally struck out and threw his helmet and began ranting in the dugout that I'd pulled a trick on him. That was the last thing on my mind. I really didn't know what was coming and I was just talking to myself. Tony Horton's a high-strung guy, and the next time up he apologized. "But it's tough enough to hit normally," he said, "without something like that to bother my concentration."

I drove in a run with a double to give us a 4-3 lead, then Cleveland tied the score, and we had to play extra innings. Sparma came in to pitch the bottom of the tenth, with the score still 4-4, Joe walked the first man, then the second batter put down a bunt that Joe, Cash, and I all went for, and nobody fielded. Joe walked the third man and with the bases loaded, they won the game on a broken-bat blooper into center field. It was the seventh game Sparma has lost in little over a month and what's more, someone stole his stereo tape recorder, a Father's Day gift, the other night. Things aren't going too well for Joseph.

Back at the hotel, my wife and I ordered dinner from room service and watched the astronauts walk on the moon.

We'd missed the last plane to Roanoke, so we had to wait for a morning flight. But sitting up in our room and watching history was a lot more gratifying than catching the plane to Roanoke ever could have been. It was amazing the way those guys were jumping around and having so much fun on the moon, acclimating so quickly. And it just made me cry when the President came out and spoke to those people from the White House. It's just unbelievable how man could accomplish something like that. I couldn't comprehend it—how things like computers and machines could be so perfected as to even allow something like that to be televised. It sort of scares me to think what things will be like twenty-five years from now.

That's how the first half of the baseball season ended for me—sitting in a room and marveling at important accomplishments, not brooding over baseball.

Still, baseball is my profession and I have to care about it. Right now, I'm not too happy with my batting average (.250), and I'm wishing I'd done a little better with my RBIs (thirty-one) and my home runs (thirteen).

But guess what?

The Orioles are slipping. They just lost their third in a row to Boston.

We're eleven games over .500. They're thirty-four games over .500, the same as they were three weeks ago.

If men can walk on the moon, we can catch the Orioles.

3

WHERE'S DENNY?

July 21

My wife and I got up at six o'clock this morning, caught a plane at 7:25, and arrived in Roanoke at 8:15 A.M. Then, after an hour's ride through beautiful mountains, we reached the farm owned by my stockbroker's father-in-law. The farm's set in a valley, with a handsome ranch house sitting up on a knoll overlooking a creek. The man who owns the spread retired from his business in Detroit a few years ago and decided that, rather than fight the city any more, he'd do what he'd always dreamed about—buy a farm.

When Pat and I arrived, he took us on a tour of the place. We saw his pond stocked with pike and rainbow trout, and we drove through some of his 2,000 acres, past the sheep and cattle, and up onto a hill. He pointed down one side of the valley, which was lush and cultivated, and said, "See, as far down as you can see, that's mine. And as far up as you can see, that's mine."

Then he showed us where they hunt deer and where they keep horses, and I said to myself, "That's me. This is my kind of life." I liked this man without even knowing him because to get out of the city and to do what you want to do is, well, money isn't worth dying for, and when you've reached a point in life where you want to do something, and you can afford it, why not do it?

We swam in the afternoon and my wife tried to catch some fish and we went on a hayride on the back of a wagon. Then, after dinner in a formal dining room, we sat on a screened porch and had a couple of drinks and watched the deer feeding in the cornfield.

I thought of how I'd like to own a place like this, or at least be able to stay here for three or four days. With the exception of me, Lolich, McLain, and Mayo, the Tigers are off until Thursday evening. When I left the guys yesterday in Cleveland, they said they'd think of me when they were on the eighteenth hole and I was at the ball park Tuesday afternoon taking batting practice. And that they'd think of me Wednesday when they were out swimming with their kids. It eats at you a little, but you still go down to an All-Star Game with tremendous pride. You get an opportunity to play with the best men in the game. As soon as it's over, these guys are your mortal enemies. But for this one game, you're pulling for each other. This is the day you're pulling for a guy to make that great play for you that he always makes against you and your teammates.

There's no financial compensation for playing in the All-Star Game. You get seventy-five dollars and flight expenses and a small gift—usually a plaque or a silver tea service—but 95 percent of the television and radio receipts go into our pension program. We have a tremendous pension program; that's one of the benefits of playing this game. And that pension can help you live comfortably some day on whatever kind of farm it is that you're dreaming about.

July 22

Early this morning, we found out that Piedmont Airlines, the only airline that flies from Roanoke to Washington, was out on strike. So at 9 A.M., with a White House reception for the ballplayers scheduled in seven hours, four of us—me, my wife, Jerry LeVan, and his wife—piled into a rented car and began driving.

We had our golf clubs with us and there wasn't enough trunk space, so we had to get a rope and tie some of the stuff on the roof. Four times between Roanoke and Washington the rope broke. Both my wife and Jerry's are pregnant, and about three-fourths of the way to Washington, my wife got carsick and we had to stop for her. Finally, at five minutes to three, we walked into the Shoreham Hotel in Washington. I was wearing white Levis, white shoes, a casual shirt, and a very worried look. The bus to the White House was leaving in half an hour and not only wasn't I dressed, I didn't even know where I'd be able to change; because of a foul-up, I didn't even have a room reservation.

Lolich and McLain had adjoining rooms at the Shoreham, and luckily I found them and went up there to change. They said they were flying out in Denny's plane tonight—right after the game—so we decided we'd take over their rooms. With that settled, I got into fresh clothes, ran to the bus, got to the White House, and was stopped at the door. I didn't have a pass. The American League, in its supreme intelligence, had sent my White House pass to Tiger Stadium, a place I haven't seen in ten days.

But they finally let me in, and after some *hor d'oeuvres* and drinks, we were ushered—and at the White House, you are *ushered*—into the East Room. President Nixon came in and spoke about his lifetime interest in baseball. Then Bowie Kuhn, the commissioner of baseball, gave the President an award for being the nation's "No. 1 Fan," and the National League president gave him a lifetime pass, and the American League president, Joe Cronin, stood in a corner, smoking a cigar. Pretty embarrassing for the American League, getting signals crossed up like that.

It began to pour outside—drumming torrents of rain—as we filed by, one by one, to shake hands with the President. I was one of the last men through, and Mr. Nixon said he'd seen me play last week against the Senators. "I've watched your career," he went on, "and admired your comeback in the Series last year." Then he said, "You played first base last week, but tonight you'll be catching."

The President was going to throw out the first ball, and I'd be catching it, so I said, "That's right. I hope you have good stuff tonight."

"Well, be alive," he said, "because I've been getting my arm in shape."

"Mr. President," I said, "the way it's raining, you might not need it tonight."

He looked up, surprised at the rain he could see out the windows. "Oh, no," he said, "it can't rain. Maybe we'll have to take this game to the Astrodome, so the rain can't affect it."

We were ushered into another room where I met Vice-President Agnew and Roy Campanella, the former Brooklyn Dodger who was paralyzed in an automobile accident. It was a thrill meeting Campanella. He and I were both catchers under the late Charlie Dressen, the manager who influenced me more than any other I played for. Roy said that Charlie had influenced him the most, too. I told Roy that Charlie was always comparing me to him, that he was always saying, "Campanella could do it, why can't you?"

I could tell Roy was happy to be talking to me, because he sort of held onto my hand while three or four people came up and introduced themselves and went on their way. He was in his wheelchair, paralyzed from the waist down, and one of the things that amazed me was his hands. They were the smallest I'd ever seen, and I wondered whether they'd gotten soft and shriveled up since the paralysis. I asked some fellows who knew him before and they said no, he'd always had small, soft hands, which is quite unusual for a catcher.

Then we got out of the White House and into a bus and over to the stadium. In the dugout, where the rain had drained off the field, the water was almost deep enough for swimming. But we weren't certain the game would be called because NBC had saved prime evening time for the telecast, so Mayo called the pitchers and catchers in for a meeting. He talked about the first couple of National League hitters, then suddenly looked up and said, "Where the hell is McLain?"

"He's out on the field," somebody said, "having his picture taken with the National League starter."

"Oh, what the hell," Mayo said. "Let's go through these hitters, anyway. Denny wouldn't pay any attention to what we're saying, anyway."

After the meeting, the game was postponed until tomorrow, and at nine o'clock we got on the American League bus and started back to the Shoreham Hotel. I figured McLain and Lolich would now be keeping their rooms and I wondered if my wife had been able to get some rooms for us or if we'd be sleeping on the floor. As it turned out, I really should have been worried about the bus ride. To avoid the crowd and save time, our driver decided to take the long way around Washington. Before very long, he'd already run into two floods and one accident and gotten lost in Alexandria, Virginia.

This bussy didn't know Washington any better than I did, and I don't live there, nor do I drive a bus around town for a living. For the first hour, I wasn't paying any real attention to what he was doing. I was sitting next to Frank Robinson, and we were chatting and we just figured he was taking a route which would get us back in pretty good shape. Then we realized he was lost. We realized it after he stopped the fourth time to ask directions. He asked in Alexandria; he asked in Arlington. He went past one Hot Shoppe restaurant four times. The fourth time, Rico Petrocelli and Mike Andrews from the Red Sox asked him to let them off at the Hot Shoppe so they could get something to eat, and to pick them up on the next run by the place.

We could see the Capitol dome in the distance and we just kept getting farther and farther away from it. One time we saw a sign: "Mount Vernon—7 miles." The bussy hit two low hanging branches on side streets. We knew how bad he was going when he asked directions from people in a car with California license plates.

The guys were agitating him hard. We accused him of getting paid by the mile. "How'd you get to be the All-Star bussy?" Carl Yastrzemski said. "You sure didn't get it on merit."

When we were going through side streets in Virginia, Paul Blair said, "Is this your old Good Humor route?"

Finally, close to 11 P.M., we got back into D.C. again and gave the driver a standing ovation. We'd been through Maryland and Virginia. "Someone is going to have to come up to my room," Frank Robinson said, "and explain that I really was on a bus ride for the past two hours. My wife'll never believe me."

We walked into the Shoreham and there were the National Leaguers; they'd been back for an hour. Luckily, my wife had gotten rooms for us, so we relaxed a bit, then went out to dinner with the Loliches and the LeVans.

McLain didn't go with us because he had a 7 A.M. appointment back in Detroit to have dental surgery. Mayo gave him permission to fly his plane back to Detroit, and I bet Denny ten dollars he wouldn't make it back to Washington in time to pitch. Frank Robinson couldn't believe Denny was actually going to do it. Denny said he was going to bring a copilot back with him, so he could get some sleep on the trip back. I told Denny I wanted to take out a $100,000 life insurance policy on him. I told him I'd pay the premiums until age fifty, and if he were still alive by then, he'd have the option of taking the cash value or picking up the premiums and changing the beneficiary to his wife. He's thinking about it. It's not a bad deal for either of us.

July 23

I had breakfast in my room today to avoid all the autograph seekers, equipment manufacturers, bubble-gum representatives, salesmen, club executives, major-league and minor-league scouts, managers, general managers, and all those other people who come to the All-Star Game.

Then I climbed on the bus. Our driver actually could find his way to the park and, after batting practice, we had a meeting with Mayo and Alvin Dark, our third-base coach, to go over signals. Reggie Jackson of Oakland had some trouble remembering the signals. He kept practicing them, going over them out loud. "Don't worry," we told him. "When in doubt, just hit a home run." Hell, he's got thirty-seven home runs already.

Denny was scheduled to be the starting pitcher, but an hour before the game he still hadn't shown up. So Mayo told Mel Stottlemyre of the Yankees he'd start if Denny didn't get there. Mel was a little nervous. "You don't have to worry about starting until thirty-five minutes before the game," I told him. "This is just par for the course for Denny."

One of the writers asked me if Denny's failure to show up surprised me. "Nothing he does surprises me," I said. Really, I can't blame Denny for this. If you've ever had trouble with your teeth, you know how it can make your whole body ache and this time he *had* made the appointment for seven o'clock in the morning on what was supposed to be a day off.

When Stottlemyre went out to the outfield to shag flies, I followed him and asked him what he wanted to do in the game—what pitches he liked to throw in certain situations. Then I discussed the same thing with the other pitchers. Blue Moon Odom of Oakland wouldn't tell me anything. He said that after last year's All-Star Game in Houston, when he'd told me how he wanted to pitch, the Tigers had bombed him the rest of the season. He said I'd told the team his secrets. He's awfully suspicious.

Mayo called a quick meeting and told the players, "We're here for one thing—to win this game. I'm going to try to get everyone in the game, but if you don't get in, I want you to understand. We are here to best represent the American League and to try and win the game." I got hold of Minnesota's Harmon Killebrew and Baltimore's Brooks Robinson, who both have receding hairlines like me, and told them to be sure to stand beside me during the introductions, so I wouldn't look so bad. They did it: a union of the "Dome Guys."

I wasn't nervous. I've never been nervous going into an All-Star Game, not like I was nervous going into the World Series last year, or into a crucial regular-season game. I didn't figure Stottlemyre would be nervous either. But he bounced two breaking balls over my head when he was warming up in the first inning (maybe it was his surprise start) and he couldn't keep the ball down the way he usually does. He gave up three runs, then Blue Moon gave up five and Denny, who arrived twenty minutes after the game started, pitched the fourth inning and gave up one. Johnny Bench of Cincinnati, who is the best young catcher I've ever seen, hit a home run for them, and Willie McCovey of the Giants hit two homers. When they had about eight runs, we got a call in the dugout from the bullpen. It was from John Roseboro, our second catcher, and Clay Dalrymple, our batting-practice catcher. Both of them had played in the National League many years and at our meeting yesterday, they'd given us a scouting report on the National League hitters. "Hey," Roseboro said now, "forget about what we told you. Use your own judgment."

Dave McNally pitched after McLain. I've never been able to figure out why I can't hit well against him because his stuff just doesn't seem overpowering at all. But now, catching him, I could see that he's a little quicker than it appears when batting against him. And he thinks real well out there and knows how to move the ball around. We were thinking alike. You could just feel that relationship developing, knowing that he was seeing the same thing about a batter that I was. The word in the meeting was to try to keep the ball in on Willie Mays. So we put a couple of fast balls in on him, then a couple of sliders that he fouled off. Then I called for a fast ball away, and Dave was right there, nodding, thinking the same way I was, because Mays was now looking for the pitch to be inside. We got Willie opening up, looking for the pitch to be inside, and the pitch was a sinking strike on the outside corner. All Willie could do was just throw his bat at the ball and hit a lazy fly to right field.

McNally pitched two shutout innings, but it was too late. They beat us, 9-3. Personally, I had a good day, knocking in two of our three runs with a home run and a single. I came out in the seventh inning, and by then Denny had packed and left the park. Mickey Lolich and his wife had flown into Washington with Denny and had expected to go back to Detroit in Denny's plane, but during the game, Denny had said, "No, you'll have to get back your own way. I've got to go to Florida."

According to Mickey afterward, Denny was pretty gruff, saying he had his "own business to tend to and the heck with you all." The night before, I'd warned Mickey to get temporary reservations on my flight back to Detroit because you never could be certain what McLain might do. Mickey had, and we all flew out together in the evening—my wife and I, Mickey and his wife, Mayo, our trainer, and one of the Detroit writers, Pete Waldmeir. On the flight, Mickey told Waldmeir about his conversation with Denny. You could see Waldmeir's eyes light up over the possibility of a good story. "You better stay away from that guy," I told Mickey, but I think I told him too late. I think we're in for a bit of controversy. Just what we need to help draw our club together for the final ten weeks of the season.

4

TIGER
FINISH

July 24

I got to the park early tonight, and Denny McLain was already there. "I got to see Mickey when he comes in," Denny told me.

Pete Waldmeir's story had been as tough as I'd expected. He'd quoted Mickey Lolich saying, "Denny never thinks about his friends or his teammates. Just himself."

"I was with Mickey on the plane and drove him to his car," I told Denny, "and he didn't seem *that* teed off to me."

"Well," Denny said, "I'm going to give him the benefit of the doubt and wait and hear what he has to say."

When Mickey came in, the two of them huddled for a few minutes until Mayo Smith called a meeting. "Denny has consented," the manager said, "to not fly his plane on days on which we have ball games."

Denny, who was sitting in the corner, said, "Now that's not exactly what we agreed to."

And Mayo shot back, "Yes. That's exactly what we agreed to."

Denny believes that the rule applies only on days when he's pitching, not on *all* playing dates.

I think the ban ought to apply to all game days and I think it will be very helpful—not so much to Denny's own work, because his pitching has remained brilliant, but to the team morale. The ban will help create more of a team feeling, help eliminate the situation we have now, where players knock Denny because he gets special privileges. And, I guess, it's got to help him a little bit on the mound, too, because with the schedule he keeps, he's got to be tired a lot of the time.

Maybe the confrontation between Mickey and Denny will be good for the team in another way, too. I think Denny and Mickey might go out this last half of the season and try to outpitch each other. In fact, Mickey pitched tonight and was just great. He struck out thirteen Kansas City Royals and we won, 3-1. His record is 14-2 and Denny's record is 14-5. We've got sixty-eight games to go, and they'll get fifteen to twenty starts each. I hope they both win twenty-five.

July 25

I think the people in Detroit have taken Mickey's side in the debate. When Denny was introduced as the starting pitcher tonight, he was booed. What the fans didn't know was that for the first time all season, Denny had showed up early, taken batting practice, and worked hard. But he just smiled when they booed him, then went out and, in an hour and fifty-nine minutes, shut out Kansas City. Fifteen for him.

July 26

We won our third straight since the All-Star Game, a 12-2 laugher for Earl Wilson, but the Orioles are keeping right with us. All I can remember is that when we got hot and won eighteen out of twenty-two a while back, Baltimore won nineteen out of twenty-four. Still, we just have to keep hoping that we can stay hot and they go flat. We're fourteen games over .500 now, our peak for the season.

Usually, in an easy win like the one today, even when some of the regulars are able to come out of the game in the middle innings, I'm reluctant to ask for a rest, too. If I come out, and then something happens to Price, Mayo would be forced to put in a guy who isn't a catcher. But today I had to ask to come out because the lower portion of my back was bothering me. When that happens, I get worried. The lower vertebrae in my back, instead of being fused, are held together by muscles. That's a birth defect that about 5 percent of the people in the country have. It's nothing to worry about, but if a man who does physical work isn't careful when those muscles start getting tired, he can put himself out of action for a while.

I was leery about making any quick movements today that might strain the muscles, and when I came out of the game, I went in for some heat therapy on my back. Last year, because of another kind of injury—a pinched nerve —I played through the end of August and all of September without any feeling in my left leg; whenever I sat for a length of time, I couldn't feel anything in my toes. This year, with all that ground we have to cover to catch the Orioles, I can't afford to have anything bothering me.

July 27

My brother-in-law, a high school sophomore, came to the locker room before the game and was amazed at the things ballplayers do to kill time. Some of the guys were working on model airplanes, some were sleeping, some were eating ice cream. Others were playing cards and some more were standing in front of the mirror, practicing their swings. A bunch of the guys were answering mail.

You get anywhere from twenty to fifty pieces of mail a day. I usually take mine home to our babysitter, who takes my presigned cards, addresses them, and sends them out for me.

Kansas City beat us, 7-2, another loss for us on a day when the rotation called for our fourth starting pitcher. Dobson was the starter today, but according to the newspapers, Kilkenny is going to be the fourth starter in our next series, against Minnesota. If the rookie could get hot, we'd be in good shape.

July 28

With an off-day today, we packed the kids into the station wagon and drove up north to the cottage. Around noon, I went over to a friend's house to pick up a lawn mower, and when I bent over to lift it up, I got the sharpest pain in my back I've ever had. I called the team physician at Henry Ford Hospital in Detroit. "Get here as fast as you can," he said.

My wife and kids were planning to stay up north the rest of the week, but now I couldn't drive home alone. So we packed everyone into the wagon again and for three and a half hours, I rode in the back seat, just about unable to move. When I got out of the car, I couldn't stand up straight, and I couldn't bend down to tie my shoe.

At the hospital, they X-rayed me and checked the medical history of my back. They won't decide what to do with me until tomorrow. I was able to move around enough to visit Dick McAuliffe, who entered the hospital during the All-Star break to have his knee looked at. They operated on Mac this morning. Even tonight, his knee was swollen so bad, he couldn't sleep. The toughest thing is to have to lie on your back, and he'll be doing that for a long time. The doctors say he's out the rest of the season. It's that kind of year.

A few other guys got hurt today, too, Mac

told me. Mickey Lolich, who works for a motor-bike company, had some of the team out to his house and they were fooling around with Mickey's motor bikes. Cash fell off and banged himself up, too. Somehow, that sounds a little more logical than getting hurt while lifting a lawn mower.

July 29

The verdict is that no bones have moved, no discs have ruptured. What I have is a strain in my lower back. To keep me from having muscle spasms, they've been giving me shots, which relax me and put me to sleep. It seems that every two or three hours, just as I'm waking up, the nurse is here to give me another shot, and I go back to sleep. I'm not very fond of needles. I'd rather go through a meat grinder in football or catch a doubleheader than get a shot. I've actually broken a few needles because my muscles have contracted—in fear—just before the shot has gone in.

McAuliffe is under sedation, too, and he's been urging them to give him even more than he's getting. He's in real pain. Like me, he hates hospitals and hates getting hurt. It's tough owning up to pain. I guess I figure if you're big and strong you should, first, never get hurt and, second, never feel pain.

Between naps, Mac and I listened to the twi-night double header from Minneapolis, with McLain and Lolich pitching for us. Their rivalry didn't help today. We lost both games, and Northrup pulled a muscle in his thigh. Now three of us are out. There's a chance I can leave the hospital tomorrow, but I won't be able to play for a while. The doctors are giving me the same advice they'd give a seventy-five-year-old man: "Take it easy and let nature take its course, and if everything works out, you'll be all right." Terrific. That seems about as brilliant to me as their habit of waking me up all the time to take my temperature. What's my temperature got to do with a strained back?

July 30

Because no other rooms were available when I checked in, the hospital put me in a suite. This morning, I heard a familiar voice coming from the other room. It was very early and I was thinking, "Oh, man, come on, Denny, if this is a dream, not you!"

I knew Denny had pitched last night in Minneapolis, and it wasn't even 7 A.M. yet.

I was lying there, trying to figure it all out, when the head of dermatology walked in. "Hey, we got a teammate of yours in here," he said. "We didn't have any other rooms, so we had to move him in here. He was acting up last night in Minneapolis, and the doctor up there checked him and said he had a slight case of pneumonia. We think he's got bronchitis and should be in the hospital."

The general manager, Jim Campbell, came by after breakfast. "With everyone in here," he said, "I'm beginning to believe I own this wing." Meanwhile, Denny kept coughing and coughing. I brought him a couple of magazines and sat with him a while, and he sounded terrible.

About ten o'clock this morning, the doctor told me I could leave the hospital. He said I had to take it easy, but he gave me a set of exercises to do every day. The exercises are designed to build up the lower back and stomach muscles. Since my vertebrae are held together by muscles, rather than being fused, the muscles must be strong or the vertebrae can slip and the muscles will tear. I've always done exercises for this over the winter and in the spring, but I've figured that in the summer the constant up and down of everyday catching would be enough exercise. Now, for the rest of my career, I'm going to have to do fifteen or twenty minutes of these exercises every day.

My wife came to the hospital to pick me up, and once I
got home, I started thinking that perhaps, since the doctor
had told me I could jog, I was well enough to rejoin the
team today. I called the doctor and told him I could jog
with the club, get sound and heat treatments, and lend a
little moral support. He checked with Jim Campbell and
told me it would be okay, as long as I didn't try to play.
"You know how I feel about guys who have minor injuries and don't even show up at the ball park," I told my
wife. "It's one thing to be in the hospital and unable to
get to the park, but it's another when you're able to make
it, but just don't come."

My wife wasn't too impressed with my decision. And
that's putting it mildly. She knows I need rest and thinks
that the best place to get it is at home. But I believe it's
easier to rest away from home, in a motel where you don't
do all those things you do running a home. With the club,
I can get more treatment and have a chance of working
myself back into the lineup sooner.

So I flew up to Minneapolis and surprised Joe Sparma.
"Who's there?" he said when I knocked on the door.

"It's me, roomie," I said.

"I thought you were in the hospital," he said.

"I just couldn't stay away from you," I told him.

"Gee, am I glad to see you," Sparma said. "I get scared
being by myself."

I got on the team bus and Mayo was surprised to see
me, too. McLain had told me that the guys were all making up stories about how I got hurt, that the story about
lifting a lawn mower just didn't sound good to them. He'd
told me Northrup had bet ten dollars that I got hurt water-
skiing, and someone else had said I got hurt running my
snowmobile on the grass. Now, as I walked on the bus, I
said, "Okay, Northrup, you lose ten bucks. I really was
lifting a lawn mower."

Northrup was in no mood to argue; he may be out of
the lineup longer than me. None of the other guys wanted

to kid around too much about injuries, either, because so many people are hurt on the club that before we went out and beat the Twins tonight, the guys were running around and calling the trainer's room "Mayo's Clinic."

July 31

Jim Kaat, the Twins' pitcher, called me about noon. He runs a promotional film company and he wanted my permission to use some film clips of me as the catching instructor in a new series they're doing. They're going to sell the films in dime stores and toy stores. The pay is pretty good—$250 for the permission and a 5 percent royalty on every print they sell. The other players involved are first-class, all big names, so I was happy to get in on the deal.

I went out after the call, bought my wife a present, then rested until it was time to go to the park. Before the game, I ran twelve wind sprints and got some heat treatment. The wind sprints didn't hurt too much. I even tried swinging a bat—mostly with my hands, not with any body pivot. Then I sat on the bench and watched Mike Kilkenny pitch his first major-league game as a starter.

Mike's a cocky guy. When he comes in from the bullpen, he'll often act as he did against Baltimore a few weeks ago. That is, he'll say, "Who's up?" and when Mayo and I tell him, he'll say, "Aw, give me the ball. He's as good as out."

Mayo and I always say, "I hope you know what you're talking about, young fellow."

Actually, big talk like Kilkenny's is a front. It's his own way of dealing with his nervousness. We all get nervous. Willie Horton has told me many times, "I shouldn't be getting nervous. I thought that after I'd been around the league a while, I wouldn't be nervous like this, but here it is again." Willie gets quiet when he's nervous. Mike talks big.

He pitched pretty well tonight, even though we were beaten, and he just might be the fourth starter we've been looking for. That would give us ideal balance in the rotation—two lefties, Mike and Mickey, and two righties, Denny and Earl. Mike's been our best relief pitcher and that would hurt the bullpen, but you've got to think of your starters first.

We flew back to Detroit right after the game, nobody in a very good mood because we'd lost three out of four to the Twins. When I got home and jumped into bed, the first thing my wife said was, "Don't you agree with me now? It would have been better for you to stay home."

I just said, "Good night, honey. It's nice to be home."

August 1

My wife and I argued all morning about my decision to spend the past two days in Minneapolis. "Listen," I told my fifteen-year-old brother-in-law, who's still visiting us, "I have nothing against your sister, but if you stay around here long enough, you're going to learn about women."

He came out to the park with me later and I got him a uniform so he could shag flies. I put on a back brace, took batting practice, and hit the ball with some authority. Then I went back to the clubhouse for some heat packs and a rubdown. Dr. Russell Wright, an osteopath who specializes in athletic injuries, took a look at me in the clubhouse. He grabbed hold of me, wrestled me, and popped a few things in my back. Just with physical force, rotating my pelvic bone, cracking everything in my back, he made me feel a whole lot better. When it comes to muscle treatment, here's one doctor who knows what he's doing. He treats you like you're an athlete, not a seventy-five-year-old man. He understands that athletes don't have time to sit back and wait for things to mend, that you have to force the issue.

Dr. Wright grabbed McLain when Denny walked into

the locker room tonight, still suffering from bronchitis, put Denny's face through contortions to open up the sinus passages, poured a decongestant down his nose, and tried to clear his chest by physical force. It was amazing that Denny should have been there at all and even more amazing that he was willing and able to pitch. Along with everything else he does that stuns me, Denny demonstrates the most unbelievable guts and recuperative powers. He came right out of the hospital today and onto the mound to start for us against the White Sox.

Northrup and I were still out of the lineup. Yesterday, along with Earl Wilson, we'd been doing a bit of second-guessing on the bench, and Northrup had been blamed for all of it. He'd really been chewed out by Mayo. Today, when the game started, Northrup didn't come to the dugout. He went to the bullpen. "I'm going to sit where I can second-guess in peace," he told me. "You and Earl and Gates and Ike can sit on the bench and get in trouble by yourself."

But in the fourth inning, Jim was back. "I can't stand it down there," he said. "Those guys are a bunch of dummies. Naragon, at one end, and McMahon, at the other, well, they're smart. But in between! It's like bookends around a bunch of garbage cans. They're the dumbest bunch of guys I've ever seen." Good old Sweet Lips.

Gates Brown and Ike Brown had a competition going in the dugout. Each of them wanted to warm up Denny between innings, so they could show the people watching on television that they were still part of the ball club even though neither's been playing much. Ike kept grabbing the catcher's mitt before Gates could get to it, so one inning I grabbed the mitt and gave it to Gates, then began rubbing him on the back and cheering him on, like a second urging on a boxer. As I was rubbing, I was fastening a funny sign on his back with bubble gum. Just as he was about to run out on the field wearing the sign, Mayo spotted it. Mayo yelled at Gates not to go out with the sign, and when Wilson and I began snickering, Mayo yelled down to us, "Quit screwing around down there." Gates didn't think it was very funny, and he went up to Ike and began poking his finger into Ike's chest. "Don't ever do that to me again," he said, "and get me in trouble with the manager. You were going to embarrass me in front of all those people."

Ike didn't know what was going on. "What did I do?" he said.

Then Gates looked over at Earl and me snickering, and he knew who was responsible. If Northrup and I don't get back in the lineup soon, we'll drive them all crazy on the bench. We won the game; it was never in doubt. McLain pitched an 8-0 shutout, his sixteenth victory. "Let me have bronchitis!" John Hiller kept shouting after the game. "Let me have bronchitis!"

August 2

I got into the game this afternoon, pinch-hitting a routine fly to center field. We were all pretty flat and the White Sox beat us, 5-0. Lolich pitched for us, and afterward he and I went to a Little League championship banquet as part of our promotional work for Dodge. This was one of my rare in-season public appearances, but it paid pretty well and, anyway, I haven't exactly been overworked lately.

On the way to the banquet, Mickey said, "How come none of the guys have come out and supported my position about McLain?"

"Why start a feud in the papers?" I said. I told him I thought his side had more merit than Denny's, but that I also felt the papers had blown the incident out of proportion. "If you want those people to write about something other than your performance on the field," I told him, "that's your prerogative. But I don't want to get involved in it."

"And maybe," I said, "it's done some good, because the management is clamping down on Denny a little bit."

Mickey acknowledged that all of that seemed to make sense, but I think he'd still like some public support. He's a sensitive guy.

August 3

I came to the park today feeling in pretty good shape and flipping a coin, saying, "Maybe I will and maybe I won't." After working out and throwing pretty good, I walked up to Mayo and told him he could use me in an emergency today and that I would be ready for sure tomorrow. He didn't need me today. Jim Price hit a home run, Willie Horton hit a grand-slam home run, and we beat the White Sox, 6-2.

August 4

Mike Kilkenny made his second start tonight, and lost again, giving up five runs to Minnesota in the first inning. The club is real lax. Maybe it's because of injuries, but mostly, I suspect, it's because the Orioles refuse to slump. At dinner the other night a man asked me, "What's really wrong with the Tigers?"

"Sir," I said, "there's only one thing wrong. And that's the Baltimore Orioles."

August 5

Not only did I play tonight, I played and played and played—thirteen innings against the Twins. Denny was our starting pitcher. His fast ball wasn't very fast, and his curve wasn't much, either. Certainly, we have no right to expect much from him these days, with that bronchitis he's fighting.

Still, he is Denny McLain. Late in the game, after he'd

given up about ten hits, he had Harmon Killebrew coming up with a couple of guys on base. The score was tied, so I went out to the mound to talk to Denny. Mayo started out, too. "I'm going to talk Mayo out of taking me out of the game," Denny said.

"You've got to be kidding me," I said. "With that junk you've got."

When Mayo reached the mound and said, "Well, I think we've seen enough." Denny said, "Nah. I've pitched over 200 innings for you. I can get out of this thing all right. You've got to give me a chance."

I'd never seen Mayo change his mind, but he did tonight. "Okay," he said, "but you'd better get out of it."

Mayo left the mound. "Now what are you going to do?" I said to Denny.

"I don't know," he said. "Maybe say the best prayer I've ever said. I've never been so scared in my life. My knees are shaking."

"I don't blame them," I said. "With that garbage you've been throwing up there."

Killebrew came up and hit a line shot right at Tommy Matchick. Then Rich Reese hit another line shot—right at our center fielder. Only McLain could do it. Two rockets, two outs.

Denny came out the next inning, and first McMahon, then Dobson, then Hiller pitched relief. I wasn't sure my back was going to hold out as the game moved into extra innings. By then, I was catching on one knee rather than in the crouch. But I was hitting pretty good—hard fly balls every time, one of them for a hit. In the thirteenth, though, with the bases loaded and none out, when all I needed was a fly ball to win the game for us, I struck out. Swinging. As if I had a hole in my bat. Luckily, Don Wert won it for us a few minutes later, with a single.

After the game, I decided that I'm going to learn Spanish during the off-season. A couple of times, with Cesar Tovar at bat for Minnesota, and Leo Cardenas in the on-deck circle, they were talking to each other in Spanish. I'd call a pitch and slide a little outside getting ready to catch it, and Cardenas may have been saying, "Be alive, the catcher is moving outside." If they're stealing anything, I want to be able to stop it. I'm going to learn the language and next year just pretend I don't understand it. This pennant is almost out of reach, so I may as well start thinking about next season.

August 6

Lolich lost to the Twins tonight, and for the third time in a row, we didn't score more than one run for him. We're all getting edgy. We can feel the end coming.

I was given a rest, so I sat out in the bullpen, where Hiller had a radio tuned to the game. Ray Lane, the Tiger radio broadcaster, said at one point that some fans in the bleachers were holding up a banner which said: "Fearsome Foursome: McAuliffe, Horton, Freehan, Kaline." The guys in the bullpen began razzing me and, between innings, I used the bullpen telephone and called the radio booth. "Why'd you go and embarrass everybody by reading that sign?" I said to Lane.

"What do you mean?" he said.

"Of those four names on the sign, only one is in the lineup tonight, and you know it," I said. "McAuliffe is on crutches, I'm in the bullpen, and Kaline's getting a rest. Lighten up. You're embarrassing me."

Guess what? Baltimore won tonight. We're fifteen games behind.

August 7

There were tornado warnings all around the state this afternoon. When that happens, it means the wind is coming in from the southwest, making it tough at the ball park for right-handed hitters to hit the long ball, and easy for lefties. We were scheduled to use a right-handed pitcher and the Twins a left-hander, giving their lefty hitters an extra edge. "Things just keep going right for us this year," I said to Mayo before the game. "If this were last year, we'd be the ones with the left-hander going."

As long as I'm discussing the little ironies of a disappointing season, there's the case of Minnesota's Rod Carew, the leading hitter in the American League. Rod Carew goes into military service tomorrow for a few days. Not three days ago, when the Twins opened a series with Detroit. Tomorrow. When the Twins open a series with the Orioles.

We won the game today, 5-3. I got three hits and knocked in the 400th run of my career, and Tom Timmerman, who is doing a consistently excellent job for us, pitched very well in relief.

We heard today that last night, in the Lindell A. C. bar, Dave Boswell, the Minnesota pitcher, was mouthing off about Billy Martin, the Twins' manager. When Bob Allison, their outfielder, tried to calm him down, Boswell reached out and slugged Allison, who had his hands in his pockets. A few seconds later, we heard, Martin came along, said, "I'll fight my own battles," and beat the hell out of Boswell. Billy always was a good street fighter. I'd like to play for him. You've got to respect that man; he can keep you on your toes and keep you hustling. He'll go out and have a couple of drinks with the boys. I like that. He can generate the day-to-day enthusiasm you need in this game. Maybe he's not the smartest manager, or the best at maneuvering, but I don't know if chess-playing managers are the best, anyway. Billy Martin has shown me a lot as a rookie manager.

August 8

Riding the bus to the ball park for our doubleheader in Chicago today, we began kidding about the pitchers who were going to start the two games for us, Sparma and Kilkenny.

"Who's pitching for us today?" someone would yell, and the answer would be a variation on the motto the 1948 Boston Braves had. The Braves used to say, "Spahn and Sain, and pray for rain." We kept saying, in the bus, "Sparma and Killer and pray for rain—before the game."

That's how much we thought of our chances, but Joe pitched six strong innings and we won the first game, and even though Kilkenny wasn't good at all in the second, we still won, 9-7. We're back to fourteen games over .500, our season peak.

On the bus before the game, Mayo had told me that Price was sick. "Don't worry," I said. "I'm prepared to do whatever's necessary." What was necessary, I figured, was for me to catch a doubleheader. I got three hits in the first game and had one in the second when, in the sixth inning, I felt something give in my back. Between innings, I grabbed Bill Behm, our trainer, and said, "C'mon, let's do some work on my back. Just rub it where I feel it's starting to go." Bill rubbed it with some hot stuff to get the circulation going, then, while I was out catching the seventh inning, told Mayo.

"It's all right," I told Mayo when I came in for the top of the eighth.

"Bill says it's not," Mayo said. "You hit and then I'm taking you out."

"Don't do that," I said. "You've no one to catch with Jimmy sick." Jimmy had been in the locker room all day, dizzy from a virus and sleeping most of the time.

"I'll catch Campbell," Mayo said. "That's what he's here for." We'd brought Dave Campbell back from the minors a few weeks ago.

"Don't do that," I said. "He's never caught except in a couple of intrasquad games."

I got a base hit and turned around, and there was Campbell coming out to run for me. I left the game, and we scored four runs to go ahead, 9-7. Now we had two innings to play, a two-run lead to protect, and no catcher. Price, though, who had awakened and had been listening to the game in the locker room, came out and said he'd catch. Mayo put him in, and even though Jimmy was wobbly, especially when he was circling under a couple of pop-ups, he managed to finish the game.

Afterward, we heard that the club had sold Don McMahon to the Giants. They'll probably give us a player for him over the winter, but the official terms of the deal now, with the trading deadline passed, are for a straight sale. McMahon's been a pretty important man for us, and a deal like this—sending a veteran relief pitcher off to a pennant contender—kind of shows us that the management has given up hope of our winning the pennant. Mayo didn't seem too happy with the deal, and John Sain, our pitching coach, seemed really upset. I just hope that the player we eventually get in this deal will be someone who can help us at one of our trouble spots. We're going to need some help.

McMahon himself wasn't happy about the deal. I rode up in the hotel elevator with him and he said he enjoyed being with the Tigers. It wouldn't be as easy to fit in with the Giants, he told me, because they're a cliquey club. There go the baseball businessmen again, peddling the bodies.

August 9

Denny McLain worked today, throwing what he'd call "mediocre garbage"—not very good, but not very bad. He had a 3-0 lead, but, eventually, on a home run by Luis Aparicio—a big, booming home run by a little man —Chicago caught us at 4-4.

When Denny was scheduled to bat the next inning, we had men on first and second. Mayo sent Cash up to pinch-hit. Denny ran to the locker room, grumbling, "How can he take me out at a time like this? He never gives me a chance to win ball games. How can he take me out after all the innings I've pitched for him?"

Before Denny could finish grumbling, Northrup scored from second on a passed ball. Minutes later, Stanley hit a three-run homer, and all of a sudden Denny didn't think Mayo'd made such a bad move. McLain could be that lucky —to come out of the game griping and end up having a guy score from second on a passed ball and pick up a win. Only McLain is going that good.

August 10

"Hey, did you hear what happened to Sain?" someone said on the bus going out to the ball game tonight.

"No," I said.

"He got fired."

John had been so upset by the McMahon deal, I found out, that he'd sounded off to the press, knocking the management. When the story was printed, an Associated Press report in which John said there was no communication between him and Mayo, Jim Campbell called John up to his suite. The general manager asked Sain if he'd been quoted correctly. John said he had. Campbell said there was nothing he could do but give John an outright release.

I'm sorry to see him go. Before the final World Series game last year, I told him, "John, maybe I won't get a chance to say good-bye to you after the Series, so I want you to know now that I've learned more baseball from you than anyone else."

I meant it. John showed me how you can get maximum performance from players and still make the game fun. He didn't put pressure on his pitchers when they were on the mound. He made the pitcher feel he was the boss out there and could do anything he wanted to do. He believed in taking a man out of a game after six innings, say, just before he tired, not only to prevent runs in that game, but also to keep the pitcher's confidence at a peak, so that he'd go into his next game with a positive attitude. John wanted his pitchers to have organized minds, to have their skills and strategies clearly in focus.

Sain's terrific at teaching techniques, too—the nuances of throwing a slider, the strategy of setting up a batter, all of that. And when John talks about pitching, he's talking about baseball in 1969, not back in 1934. He's not saying, "Well, I used to have a pitcher who did this or that." He's talking about current players and current psychology and current problems. If I ever become a manager, I'm going to call John Sain the day I get the job and talk to him all day about human insight.

I guess it's true John had trouble communicating with Mayo. We players always wondered why the two of them didn't communicate better. If John said the same things to Mayo he said to us, there shouldn't have been any problem. Both of them had good credentials. Since Mayo became our manager, we'd had one second-place finish and one World Championship; in the 1967 and 1968 seasons put together, no other American League team won as many games as we did. You'd think, with Mayo and John both dedicated to victory, they'd have been a perfect pair.

I guess it came down to this: John would have liked a big voice in decisions involving the pitchers, and Mayo, rightfully, figured that his job depended on how well we play and he wanted the final say about the pitchers. There ought to have been some middle ground they could have moved to, but instead they just kept moving farther apart.

Maybe John ought to be a manager. I think he has the ability to be a good one. People tend to think he can get along only with pitchers, but I think he gets along with everyone. The only thing I ever heard the nonpitchers complain about was John's refusal to make his pitchers run. But how can you fault him? Since John got here, very few pitchers have had arm problems. I don't know if John wants to get back into baseball, but if he does, he'll get a job. As a pitching coach for the Yankees, Twins, and Tigers, he's been in the World Series five out of the last seven years. You won't find another coach or manager who's been there that often.

Mickey Lolich beat the White Sox tonight, his fifteenth victory. I got eight hits in the Chicago series and kicked my average up into the .270s. We're sixteen games over .500 now, and we've won five straight games. But guess what? Baltimore's won four straight. We're still fourteen and a half behind.

August 11

Before tonight's game against California, the newspapermen were asking questions about the firing of John Sain. Nobody wanted to stick his neck out on that, and when a TV guy asked McLain if he'd do a filmed interview, Denny said, sure, but no questions about Sain. The TV guy agreed. Then the first question he asked was what did Denny have to say about the fight between Mayo and Sain. Denny answered with a few choice words that made the film definitely unfit for home viewing. "I warned you not to ask me about that," Denny said.

Tonight was Family Night, an event we have about three or four times a year. It's a marvelous idea. Normally, if a man wants to take his wife and, say, four kids to a game, it costs him at least fifteen dollars before he's even bought a hot dog. It's been figured that each person spends roughly a dollar and a half on refreshments for the game, which brings the cost of the evening up to twenty-five dollars, pretty expensive. On Family Night, the head of a household gets in for $2.70 and each additional person in the party for fifty cents. We always draw well on Family Nights and I think major-league baseball ought to hold them more often, particularly, when two teams who wouldn't ordinarily attract a good crowd are playing. Baseball has to work at bringing in young people, at building fans for the future. We got 32,000 people in tonight for the California Angels.

We lost, 3-1. It was a rough game. In the seventh inning, their catcher, Tom Egan, was up and Earl Wilson curved him away twice for strikes. In a situation like that, I expect the batter to begin leaning over the plate, expecting another pitch on the outside. Then I like the pitcher to come inside with a fast ball, wasting it, keeping the hitter off-balance and setting him up for an outside curve on the following pitch.

Earl's fast ball tailed in too close. It hit Egan on the cheekbone, right under his left eye. I don't believe I've ever heard a more sickening sound. The first thing I thought of as I saw Tommy lying on the ground was the ball that almost blinded Tony Conigliaro. I also thought of how fortunate I've been in never getting hurt badly when I've been hit.

Tommy lay there. "My eye, my eye," he kept saying. "What's wrong with my left eye? I can't see out of my left eye. Somebody do something." The trainer ran out and put Tommy on a stretcher, and they took him to the hospital. Later, we heard that his lack of vision was due to a nerve which had been numbed from the blow, but that he was going to be okay.

I was sick to my stomach. All the fight was out of me. I felt like stopping the game right then. Earl felt just as bad. But you have to pitch inside; that's part of the game. The Angels' coach, Rocky Bridges, who was standing there with us, said so too. Still, I hate to see anybody get hit in the eye.

August 12

Mike Kilkenny's wife gave birth to his first child, a son, at noon today. Then Mike won his first game as a starter tonight. He had two speeds on his curve ball, a good fast ball, struck out ten Angels, pitched a complete game, and showed us he can be that fourth starter we've been looking for. I'm afraid it's a little late.

August 13

I went to the Angels' locker room before tonight's game to check on Tommy Egan. I found out that Egan can see a little better now and that it looks like everything'll be all right in time. There's no damage to the eye itself, but the cheekbone's fractured and Egan'll have to be operated on. At the least, he's out the rest of the year.

Then, at the batting cage, Jim Fregosi, the Angel shortstop, and I were kidding Northrup. "When was the last time you hit a home run?" Fregosi said.

"I haven't hit one since we were in Kansas City before the All-Star Game," Northrup said. A little while later, of course, Sweet Lips hit one. He always seems to hit well when McLain is pitching. He and Denny don't get along well off the field—they agitate each other real good—but Jimmy always seems to hit the long ball for Denny and drive in runs for him.

Denny shut out the Angels, 3-0. "I'm just working for a raise now," he said afterward. He said Mayo told him that after winning thirty-one last year, Denny had to win between eighteen and twenty-three this year to consider the season a personal success. He's got eighteen victories, and the way he figures, he's already done his job. He's in first place, and only the rest of us are in second.

August 14

We were off today, and I was able to play golf. I shot a 79, playing with my dad and a couple of other people involved in our mobile-home operation in Florida. We combined business and fun, holding a board of directors meeting out at the country club, then playing golf, and finally having dinner with our wives. Pat and I left early, so that she could get home and pack. She and Sparma's wife are coming along tomorrow on our road trip to play the three West Coast teams. Even a jinx can't harm us this year.

I wish we were in the American League's Western Division. Our record is 66-49, and that would put us right up there in the pennant race in that division. In fact, we'd be right up there in any division in either league, except the one we're in.

In the Eastern Division of the American League, only one team is under .500, and yet we're all bums because of Baltimore. I read that Hank Bauer, who was fired last year as the Orioles' manager, recently criticized Earl Weaver, his successor, for being a push-button manager. "I may be a push-button manager," Weaver answered. "but at least I'm pushing the right buttons." He sure is. They're still playing over .700.

August 15

On the way out to Oakland, my wife suggested, "Why can't someone hijack this plane? Hawaii would be nice this time of year." We should have been hijacked. We lost to the A's, and my hitting streak, which had reached ten games, was broken. It seems like we always lose the first game we play on the West Coast. When you get to the seventh, eighth, and ninth innings and you reach back for that reserve energy, you don't have it. It may only be eleven o'clock Oakland time, but back in Detroit, where you've been living for weeks, it's one in the morning.

August 16

At the batting cage today, I saw Danny Cater, who hadn't gotten a hit in his last eleven at bats. "Don't worry, Danny," I said, "We'll take care of you."

Northrup came by. "Don't worry, Danny," he said. "We'll get you back up to .280."

We moved away then, because they were having a home-run hitting contest before the game. Our representatives were Horton and Cash. Oakland sent up Reggie Jackson and Sal Bando. Jackson, who's leading the major leagues with forty-two home runs, is a good guy—he gave me a pack of his favorite sunflower seeds yesterday—and a strong guy; with that dead air they have in the Oakland stadium at night, it's amazing that he's been able to hit all those home runs. I figured he'd win the home-run contest, and so did everyone else, but we were wrong. Horton did. Not that it mattered to anyone. There was a seventy-five-dollar prize to the winner of the contest, and twenty-five dollars each to the other three, but, as usual in those contests, the participants all got together beforehand and agreed to pool the money and split it evenly.

Blue Moon Odom started for Oakland. We like to beat him. We've had a couple of fights with Oakland over the last couple of years, and Blue Moon always seemed to be sneaking up behind somebody and slugging or kicking him, which doesn't make him very popular with us. About the only consolation we had after losing the game tonight was that Blue Moon didn't get the win. We knocked him out of the game.

We lost in the bottom of the tenth. We picked up a one-run lead in the top of the tenth, then Danny Cater, naturally, doubled in the tying and winning runs.

Afterward, my wife and I got into the car the Dodge people are letting me use out here and did some touring—Sausalito, Fisherman's Wharf, the Golden Gate Bridge. At dinner, we ran into Raymond Berry, the former football player. My wife's dad was a great fan of Berry's when Raymond was catching passes and making incredible moves for the Baltimore Colts, and my wife was impressed by meeting him. "Why don't you get me his autograph?" she said, after we sat down at our table.

"Let's just leave it alone," I said. "Let's just sit here."

August 17

Denny is now calling himself "The Irish God." He says his Irish luck never runs out. He's got everybody believing it, too. Wilson and Lolich just laugh when Denny pitches because they know that by the fourth inning he's going to get a bunch of runs. His arm was stiff tonight and he didn't have his good stuff and he had to struggle. But Kaline hit two home runs, Wert, Northrup, Stanley, and Tresh hit one apiece, and Denny won his nineteenth game.

I got hurt in the ninth inning. With the bases loaded for Oakland, Bert Campaneris hit a ball to Wert. Donnie threw to me to force Tommie Reynolds at home, and I moved up to the edge of the infield grass and planted my left leg in case I had to make a throw. Reynolds took a cheap shot at me. He caught me hard as I was standing there, after the play, and my knee crumpled.

I don't know if I'll be able to play in Seattle tomorrow. A catcher has to have his knees in shape to make those up and down movements, and the thought of a knee injury has always frightened me. I'm pretty teed off at Reynolds. I don't mind if people play hard. It's part of the game for a guy to hit me as hard as he wants as long as there's a play. But I hate to take a cheap shot.

Denny has his own grudge in Oakland. Their organist was at it again, booming out the music while Denny was in the middle of his windup. The guy was doing it even more than usual today because Charles O. Finley, the A's owner, was at the ball park. It seemed as if the organist was trying to show off for the boss. Whenever Denny got into the top of his windup, the organist would play, and Denny would back off. Then the organist would play, "Oh, Danny Boy," in a taunting way. "Everytime that organist played," Denny told the writers, "I expected the center-field scoreboard to open up and Charlie O. to come riding in with a bunch of elephants. And I don't mean Charlie O., the Oakland mule. I mean Charlie O., the other donkey. That organ player makes me feel like I'm leading a three-ring circus."

Just then, Wally Moses came along and said, "I've played this game all my life. It's too bad some musician can ruin it."

Before the game, Denny had gone around and shook everyone's hand. "I want to say good-bye now," Denny said, "in case I don't have a chance to see you after the game." He wasn't scheduled to pitch in Seattle, and he was joking about not being on the plane after the game. But Mayo has been clamping down on Denny a little bit, and Denny was on that plane, up in the cockpit with me a great deal of the time, watching the pilot work.

Mayo, John Hiller, and Dick Tracewski stayed behind in Oakland. They have to testify in a court hearing. Last year, we had a fight with the Athletics in Oakland, and after the fight somebody in the stands dumped beer on one of our players. In a fit, one of our guys picked up a baseball and threw it at the fan, but the guy ducked and the ball hit a woman in the face. She's suing the Oakland club and ours for $100,000. Some of the previous witnesses have named Hiller and Tracewski as the guilty players, so they have to be in court. But neither of them did it and when they left today, we were calling each of them "Ratso" —after Ratso in the movie, *Midnight Cowboy*—and saying that they were going to court to rat on the guy who threw the baseball.

August 18

With no game scheduled, the Sparmas and the Freehans took a boat trip from Seattle into Puget Sound and up to Vancouver Island and the city of Victoria. It was a long trip, especially for my wife who's five months pregnant, but it was beautiful. I love to travel, to see different places and different life styles. I'm particularly interested in history, geography, and geology. When we fly, I always pay attention to the different soils and rock formations and water formations. And today, on the boat, I was awed by the strong, raw beauty of this area.

If I were ever traded to Seattle, I think I could learn to love this country.

August 19

The Seattle ball club has been having its difficulties—on the field and off. They charge high ticket prices—$7.50 for the most uncomfortable, rusty tin folding chairs conceivable—and they're playing in an old stadium that isn't even a good minor-league park. As a result, they're only drawing about 10,000 people a game, which is pretty unusual for a city's first major-league season.

This ought to be good territory for big-league baseball, but the future doesn't look too bright. Seattle was awarded an American League franchise on the condition that a domed stadium be built, but the voters passed a referendum for only $40 million, probably not enough for a domed stadium with today's construction costs. "I think we're having a tough time making ends meet," Ray Oyler, my ex-teammate, was telling me before the game today.

In the game, I played first. I never couldn't caught the way my knee was acting up on me. I think I've something more seriously wrong than I want to admit. Perhaps a torn ligament, or a torn tendon. I played 155 games each of the last two seasons, but I'll be lucky if I play 140 this year. First my nose, then my arm, then my back, and now my knee.

We won the game 5-3, another victory for our fourth starter, Mike Kilkenny. Afterward, Tom Timmerman went out on a blind date. He's been dating an airline stewardess here in Seattle, but when he talked to her the other day, she told him she'd be out of town today. Tom's got a lot of guts: he asked her to get him a date with another stewardess. She said okay and gave him a telephone number. Tom called the number, made a date, and tonight when he went to pick up the girl, a fat, really remarkably unattractive girl came to the door.

"Are you Judy?" Tom said.

"Yes," she said.

"Do you know who I am?" he said.

"No."

"Well," Tom said. "I'm Tom's friend. He asked me to tell you he's going to be late and doesn't even know if he's going to be able to make it."

Then Tom took off. He doesn't have *that* much guts.

August 20

My wife wanted to look over some of the stores in Seattle today, so I waved at my wallet and said, "Take some money and browse around and buy some things for the kids." I figured she'd take about twenty dollars, but she took a hundred and came back loaded with gifts for the kids, the baby-sitter, and herself. For me, a new town offers up a chance to see another corner of the world. For my wife, it's a chance to see another department store.

I went out to the park early for some ice and sound treatment on the back of my left knee. Mayo came up and asked how I felt. "I can't bend down without it hurting," I said. He turned around and walked out, not saying a word.

Then Mickey Lolich came by. Mickey was born and raised in the Northwest, and his parents were coming to the game to see him pitch. He was especially eager to do well. "You've got to catch tonight," he said. "Price and I haven't been getting along too well lately."

He wasn't really knocking Price. It's just that he and Jimmy haven't been thinking the same way lately, and Mickey and I have been working together since 1963. You learn a lot about a man in seven years—how to boost his confidence, how to tell when his stuff is a fraction off, how to compensate for that. Jimmy just hasn't been here long enough to develop that kind of rapport with Mickey. When I first broke in with the Tigers, the regular catcher was Gus Triandos. There were a couple of pitchers on the club then who always wanted him, not me, to catch them. They didn't want a young kid to come along and possibly affect their chances with inexperienced thinking.

I went to the trainer and said, "C'mon, let's try taping it up real tight." He did and, even though I couldn't bend down all the way, the tape seemed to give me enough support to play. "I think I can play with the tape on my knee," I told Mayo. "It doesn't hurt as much this way. If you want to play me, knowing that, I'll go as far as I can. But I'm not going to slide into second base to break up any double plays."

"Let's play that way," Mayo said. I was surprised. I thought he'd say, "No, we'll play the other guy."

Then I went to Mickey. "If you want me to catch," I said, "you better not complain about any passed balls." I couldn't move laterally, and if I had to dive and block a pitch with both knees together, I probably wouldn't be able to get up.

I caught the game with my left leg out and slightly off-balance. Mickey didn't throw a ball in the dirt. He had excellent control and good stuff and he beat them, 4-3. I not only survived: I even got a couple of hits.

August 21

Freehan's Second Law—the first was: Never Beat Yourself, which we violated too often this year—is: Always play an expansion club, or a very weak team, toward the end of July and through August, if possible. That's when the initial feeling that anything is possible has disappeared, and the late feeling of excitement generated by the minor-league kids trying to impress people has not yet appeared. It's happened to Seattle. There's no enthusiasm.

We beat the Pilots again, our third straight over them and our fourth victory in a row. I got two more hits, and I even won eighty-six cents later, playing gin rummy on the plane to Los Angeles. I don't usually play cards. On my first major-league trip, right after I signed for my big bonus, I walked onto the plane and up to a poker game. "Hey, kid," one of the guys said, "c'mon in. You got some money." My answer was probably the best thing I did in my first few months with the Tigers. "Naw," I said. "I'll just stand here and watch." I didn't know much about poker and it's very expensive to start from scratch and learn. Those guys knew how to play cards. On this club, Dobson's the shark. And it seems he's always got a couple of fish. He keeps saying he's just lucky. Sure. Lucky to find the fish.

August 22

Denny McLain went on the pregame television show in Anaheim today and talked about his paint company. He went on the postgame show and talked about his paint company. In between, he beat the Angels, and became the first pitcher in the major leagues to win twenty games this year. "Denny's going to write a book this winter," Cash said. "He's going to call it, *How to Win Twenty Without Breaking a Sweat.*"

We've won five in a row, twelve out of fifteen, and we're twenty games over .500. And we're still fifteen games behind Baltimore. It's so frustrating.

August 23

That little extra drive, our incentive, is gone. We were beaten today, 5-2, in a game we probably wouldn't have lost if we were in the pennant race. We're professionals and we go out and do our jobs, but we aren't able to reach back and find the extra spark we needed in the suffocating heat we played in today. Right now, the guys are making their salary drives—not sacrificing themselves for the team, but boosting their own statistics so they can use them to argue for more money in contract negotiations. We have pride—we'd rather come in second, say, than third—but it's human nature not to sacrifice yourself as much when battling for second place as for first. After our lethargic play today, I'm saying to myself, "Why didn't I push myself? You big dummy, why didn't you try to generate some enthusiasm in the rest of the team? That's your job." But, really, words can only accomplish so much. They can't turn on enthusiasm the way the possibility of getting into a World Series can.

August 24

Bowie Kuhn, the commissioner of baseball, was at the game today, watching us lose to the Angels. I like strong people, men who don't beat around the bush, who move right in to solve problems, and the commissioner is that kind of man. He's a fan and he knows the inner workings of baseball, too, and the combination has helped him make moves for the overall good of baseball, not just for the good of the owners. He just might protect the future of this game.

August 25

I spent the day in Detroit, lounging around with my kids and my parents, gathering my strength. In the next twenty-seven days, starting tomorrow night, we have thirty games scheduled without a day off. We're fourteen and a half games behind the Orioles. They've suddenly lost three in a row, and Boog Powell and Paul Blair are out with injuries. Maybe. Maybe.

August 26

I drove my wife and my kids out to the land my dad and I have bought for our campground franchise, Kampgrounds of America. My wife hasn't been too enthusiastic about my forming a corporation basically funded by my dad and me. But we have the experience because of the two Florida mobile-home parks we're involved in, and when she saw this land—eighteen pretty acres just off the interchange forty-five minutes from Detroit—she was impressed. We're planning to make a lake on the back part of the property and by the winter we should have the foundations up and part of the construction done on our lake and maybe by June 1, 1970, have eighty to one hundred sites developed for use by campers.

At the park later, we lost the first game of a double-header to Oakland, 8-6. McLain started and when he left, complaining of a sore arm, the crowd booed. Horton was also booed, very hard. It seems to me that when a man has put out hard, and you could see Horton giving 110 percent, you shouldn't boo him for physical failure. One of the reasons I have some success as a catcher is that I try to understand what goes through people's minds, and I know for certain that what's going through a man's mind when he's failed at something can't be helped by booing. It makes more sense psychologically to try to give him some encouragement and understanding if you expect him to be in the right frame of mind the next time he's facing a challenge. Anyway, we came back in the second game and, on some hot hitting by Mickey Stanley, beat the A's.

And guess what?

The Orioles lost again. Miracles, anyone?

August 27

Stanley, Northrup, Wilson, and I spent a few hours at the state fair today, holding a baseball clinic for Vernor's

Bottling, the soft-drink company I represent. About two-thirds of the audience was female.

It's amazing that so many girls react to ballplayers almost the same way they react to rock-and-roll stars. As you sign autographs, they're rubbing at you, stealing the pockets off your pants. Every mother or daughter wants to kiss you. They give you all sorts of presents. One girl wanted to give me a dog today. When you're having an off-year, it's awfully good for your ego. Maybe appearances like that ought to be mandatory for a man—or a team—in the middle of a slump.

Mike Kilkenny shut out the Athletics tonight, a superb piece of pitching. For me, the game offered one of those rare, exhilarating experiences that comes when the catcher for the first time gets into an exact groove with a pitcher, knows that from now on he understands precisely that pitcher's patterns, skills, and psyche.

It's taken the whole season for Mike and I to come together like this, each of us learning a little about the other game by game, Mayo helping me to understand Mike, too. It's easy to catch a guy mechanically, to know how to handle his fast ball, to know what his curve ball can do. But it's difficult to understand the guy psychologically, to know the little things he does to throw himself out of a groove, and to know what to do to help him.

The pieces all came together tonight. One time Mike walked Tito Francona on four pitches, then threw ball one to the next batter. I called time-out real quick; this is exactly the kind of situation, I've learned, where Mike starts getting down on himself and losing his rhythm. I walked out and said, "Now, Michael." He was starting to let his emotions show, kicking around and stomping at the dirt. "Right here," I said, "is where you're going to have to get yourself back together. Just settle down for a minute. Take a deep breath. Relax. This is where you've got to be a pitcher, not a thrower. This is where you'll be able to feed your family—by getting yourself straightened out in situations just like this. The one thing you don't want to do is lose control of everything you've got right here. Don't be rushing yourself and hurrying your windup. Just settle back and forget about walking that guy and forget about that first pitch you threw him. Let's work on getting you back to the groove you were in. Settle down and let's go at it from here on in."

Mike took a deep breath. "Okay, now I'm ready," he said. "Let's go."

I walked back in, and Mike got out of the inning with a double-play pitch.

Through the game, I'd call a pitch and he'd be right there, thinking the same way, setting up the batters, getting them out in a planned pattern. All I had to do was establish the pattern early in the game, building it, of course, on the skills he had, and he was with me the rest of the way, his confidence and success growing pitch after pitch.

I sat in front of my locker afterward feeling even more satisfied than if I'd gone four-for-four. Grover Resinger came over to me. "Young fella," he said, "you don't know it, but you caught a hell of a game tonight."

"You know what, Grover?" I said. "I thank you. But I do know it. Because tonight that boy and I were working on the same frequency. He and I were doing things that it's fun to do."

August 28

Jim Northrup went six-for-six tonight, six consecutive hits, the last one a towering home run over the roof in the bottom of the thirteenth inning that won the game for us and may have killed Oakland's pennant chances.

The A's started this series only a game and a half behind the Minnesota Twins, but after losing three out of four to us, they're three and a half behind, and plummeting.

Some of us were talking to the A's manager, Hank

Bauer, before the game. Hank's got a tough, jagged, battle sergeant's face that's been described about a million times as looking like "a clenched fist." He had on those white baseball shoes the A's wear, and one of our guys said, "You know, that head of yours just doesn't go with those shoes."

But Hank wasn't laughing the way he used to when we knew him as a ballplayer and as manager of the Orioles. Mayo said it's not only because the A's were slumping, but mostly because when you work for Charlie Finley, you never have as much fun as you do working for other owners. "Finley's always calling you at eight o'clock in the morning," Mayo said, "and staying on you all day."

The A's couldn't break their slump tonight, but Bauer had his guys battling. One time Tresh threw home on a ground ball, and I got the ball with Reggie Jackson tearing into me. Reggie, who was a halfback in high school, decided not to slide, but to run me over. We had some kind of collision, but I held the ball, and after the game, in the Lindell A. C. bar, Reggie came over and apologized for running over me. "You know I had to do it," he said.

"Hey, man," I said, "that's the game. I don't get mad when you try to do something like that. That's only your job, to try and score that run." Shoot, there was a play on. It wasn't like that cheap shot that Reynolds took at me. I like Reggie. I don't think he's going to hit sixty home runs this year, but maybe he will someday. He's a bull of an athlete.

August 29

Mayo gave me a rest against Seattle today, and I spent the game in the bullpen. When Fred Lasher began reading some statistics on the Seattle club, I said, "When you're done, why don't you send those down here? I'd like to look at a couple of things."

Fred sent them down. He made a paper airplane out of

one of the stat sheets, and flipped it toward me. It hit Sparma in the eye. Joe's been sick for a couple of weeks, and he hasn't been playing much, so he wasn't exactly in a joking mood. He got up and cursed Lasher, and he wasn't fooling. Lasher threw a punch at him.

Hal Naragon, the bullpen coach, leaped up and said, "Is this for real?" Then he broke it up. We had a new pitcher in the bullpen, a kid named Gary Taylor just up from Toledo, and when things quieted down, one of the guys said, "Welcome to the major leagues, Gary. You know how you hear about people fighting for a job? Well up here, they take it literally."

In the locker, Cash said he was going to be a fight promoter during the winter. "I got a double bill now," he said. "Lasher and Sparma, Boswell and Martin."

We could hear Mayo, in his office, getting all over Naragon for breaking up the fight between two guys who were already in the doghouse. "Let those guys go at it," Mayo was saying, "and then we'll have room on this roster for somebody else."

I don't know what Mayo is so angry about. We beat Seattle for our fourth straight win, and the Orioles lost two. I believe I'm thinking of the pennant again.

I'm thinking of the way the Baltimore Colts blew the Super Bowl and the way the Baltimore Bullets blew their chance at the National Basketball Association championship. I'm starting to think, "You know what? Maybe it could happen in three sports." We're eleven games behind them in the loss column, which is practically impossible to make up in one month, but it's funny how you get this wild hope in sports. I guess it's because we've read all those fiction books when we were kids—about how the All-American boy comes back and wins against the largest odds in the world.

August 30

We won again, 4-3, Denny's twenty-first victory. I knocked in the winning run—with a double—and I can't remember the last time I did that.

Right before I hit the double, those fibrillations—those accelerated heartbeats—started up. They kept going all the time I was on base and while I caught the next inning. When we came back to bat again, the team doctor put ice on my heart and on the back of my neck, but they didn't stop. The doctor said to Mayo, "You better get somebody else in there."

"Naw, let me go," I said. "If I can't make it, I'll let you know. I won't take any chances."

I ran out, caught Denny's last warm-up pitch, and as I reached back to throw to second base, the racing stopped.

August 31

Earl Wilson won his twelfth game today, our sixth in a row, our longest winning streak of the season.

My kids came to the game and even though they don't know everything that's going on out on the field, they can recognize me. They know I'm the guy who has on the mask, the shin guards and the chest protector, and wears his hat backwards.

My youngest daughter, Kelley, who is a little bit of a tomboy, always goes around with a baseball cap on—in the house and playing catch with her friends in the backyard. Kelley always wears her cap backwards.

September 1

Willie Horton is suddenly unbelievable. He hit a home run in each half of the doubleheader at Kansas City this afternoon, making five straight games in which he's hit home runs. We won the first game to stretch our streak to seven, then lost the second in the bottom of the ninth. The Orioles are hot again. They beat Chicago, 8-0.

September 2

The Kansas City Royals have a bunch of their minor-league players up now, a bunch of little guys who hustle like hell and hit little grounders through the infield and pop little bloopers that fall right in front of our outfielders. The bloopers beat us today, and I said to the home-plate umpire, "I'm going to send each of them a box of Wheaties over the winter, so that next year, when they hit the ball, they hit it hard enough for our outfielders to catch it."

September 3

Denny McLain has been in Detroit with his wife, who's in danger of having a miscarriage, but he showed up in Kansas City this afternoon to pitch. "Here I am boys," he said. "You're saved."

We gave Denny a standing ovation and introduced ourselves. Then he walked out to the mound, and Willie Horton hit two home runs for him, I hit one, and he had a 4-1 lead.

With that lead, Denny got two strikes on Joe Foy in the sixth inning and yelled, "I bet you can't hit the sidearm fast ball." Then Denny dropped down, threw a sidearm fast ball, and Foy hit the ball out of the park. As Foy was rounding third, he peeked at Denny and said, "Hey, I bet you I can."

I ran to the mound. "You sonuvagun," I said. "We better not lose this game by one run. You better bust your tail or you better not get on that bus after the game."

Denny sort of smiled, then shut them out the rest of the game. Afterward, on the flight back to Detroit, he didn't stop razzing us. None of us resented his absence earlier on this trip—his wife, after all, was sick, and he didn't miss a pitching turn—but we did resent the razzing. He just had to laugh and tell us that he never spent a night in Kansas City all season. All the regulars are figuring that once the season is settled, once we've clinched whatever place we're going to finish in, we ought to get back at him.

On a night he's scheduled to pitch, maybe the eight regulars will call in and say we can't come to the park, each of us using one of the excuses Denny has used this year. I don't know if we'll do it, but we sure have been talking about it. Of course, that kind of attitude doesn't help a team win pennants.

Anyway, tomorrow's our last chance for the pennant. The Orioles come into Detroit for a four-game series, leading us by twelve and a half games. If we beat them four straight the lead will be cut to eight and a half games. After that, we'll have twenty-three games to play, the last three in Baltimore.

September 4

We got home runs from Tresh and Kaline tonight and led the Orioles, 4-1, going into the ninth inning. All we had to do was get three guys out, and the game'd be over. The first one up was Frank Robinson.

Earl Wilson had struck out Frank with a fast ball down the middle once and had gotten him two other times with breaking balls. I didn't want Earl to be too careful with Frank, to take a chance on walking him. I wanted him to get a quick strike, to get an edge. I figured Frank wouldn't be swinging at the first pitch with his team behind by three runs. I figured that just this once I'd call for a fast ball, down and in, surprise him by flinging that first pitch right to his power. I figured wrong.

Earl threw the ball down and inside, and Robinson swung and hit a low line drive that just kept going. It cleared the fence by a foot.

Now we had a two-run lead, with Boog Powell up. Earl

got two strikes on Boog, who has a bad ankle. On the second strike, Boog took a big swing and twisted his ankle. He was hobbling around quite a while, trying to get himself back together. Boog's an old friend of mine—we played high-school ball against each other—and I said, "Hey, Boog, you're just playing that Jimmy Brown trick on me." You know, Jim Brown always sort of struggled back to the huddle, as if he were hurt, and then he'd run thirty-five yards and kill you. Boog just smiled and got back in the batter's box.

I called for a breaking pitch, away from him, and Earl put it in just right. But Boog got his bat around and hit a low line drive toward right field. Kaline went back for the ball and leaped, and it just went over his glove for another home run.

We were still leading by a run, and we had their two toughest hitters behind us. I saw Mayo coming toward the mound, and I ran out before he got there. "Earl," I said, "how you feeling?"

"I'm tired," he said.

"Hey, man," I said. "You been getting these guys out good all night. You know you're still throwing good. They just hit good pitches."

Mayo reached the mound. "I don't have any intention of taking you out, Earl," the manager said. "Those guys just hit good pitches. There's nothing you can do about it. Let's just get those guys the way you've been getting them out all night. Forget the home runs."

I walked back behind the plate and called a fast ball low and away on Brooks Robinson. Earl threw it perfectly for a strike. I would have liked to follow with a fast ball inside because that's the last pitch in the world Brooks would expect, but that would also be the pitch he'd have the best chance of hitting for a home run. I couldn't risk it. Brooks is a good breaking-ball hitter, too, and with Earl tiring, I couldn't take a chance on him hanging a curve. So I called for another fast ball away. Earl threw it, and

Brooks hit the ball into the upper deck, tying the score. Frank Robinson. Boog Powell. Brooks Robinson. Not a bad lineup.

I was stomping around and cursing myself as Wilson left the ball game. When Timmerman came in to replace him, all I could say to Tommy was, "Listen, the game's tied. Come on, you can win yourself a game. Just get those guys out, and we got a chance to score a run. We've got three right-handers coming up against a left-handed pitcher."

Dave Johnson hit a good breaking ball for a double, Ellie Hendricks moved him to third on a sacrifice fly and, with our infield in, Mark Belanger hit a high chopper. As we waited for the ball to come down, Johnson scored. A Tiger Finish—for Baltimore.

That was it. We went down one-two-three in the bottom of the ninth. I was three. I hit a shot to short, and Belanger flopped on his belly, knocked it down, pounced on the ball, and threw me out.

In the locker room, I sat on my stool for fully five minutes. Then I looked around and said, "You know, if I had to go back and do the same thing, I'd probably call the same pitches again."

A catcher can't second-guess himself. Mayo may have shortcomings as a manager—all managers do—but one of the things I really like about him is that he never second-guesses signal-calling. I've had managers who have called signals from the bench and inevitably we've had big losing streaks while they were doing it.

The mood of the locker room was weird. You'd have expected everyone to be completely disheartened. But we weren't. Mostly we were just smiling dumbly, stunned but accepting what had happened. I think that the words running through my mind were the words running through everybody's: "Well, guys, you know how many times we did that to people last year. Today we had it done to us. They beat us with a burst that's hard to believe, but that's the way they've been winning all year. That's the kind of club they have: Power, Speed, Pitching, Fielding, Depth. You just have to respect them. We didn't beat ourselves. They beat us."

Now it's magic-number time. The Orioles' magic number is thirteen. Any combination of Tiger defeats and Oriole victories totaling thirteen will irrevocably and officially eliminate Detroit from pennant contention. Baltimore will clinch the Eastern Division championship of the American League.

September 5

I had a meeting with the Dodge boys this morning, and when I got to their parking lot, the attendant said, "What happened last night?"

"They beat us," I said. "They've got a good baseball team, and that's all there is to it."

"Mayo should have known to take Wilson out of there," the attendant said. "He was getting tired."

"Wilson wasn't that tired," I said, "and Mayo wasn't thinking of taking him out because he wasn't that tired, and don't be saying that because you don't know what you're talking about." But I was smiling as I talked because, as annoying as those kind of questions can seem, it's still great to see the people in this town so interested in the team.

I went up to the Dodge offices, and some of the secretaries came over. "What happened last night?" they wanted to know. Then some more people came over, and asked the same question. I walked into an office to see the man I report to at Dodge and I said, "Hey, man, the last thing I want to talk to you about is last night. Let's talk about business or something else or the team in general or our chances for next year, but not about last night." He knew what I meant.

I renewed my contract with Dodge for another year.

They were happy that I was still interested in them, and I was equally happy that they were still interested in me. As part of my contract, they'll provide me with two cars again for the year, and since I'd already seen the 1970 models, I knew what I wanted. I ordered a Charger and a station wagon. Real fine machines. If people have the money and the mood to buy cars this year, Dodge is going to do just fine.

I got out to the park early. Usually the visiting team doesn't show up on the field until 5:00 or 5:15, but the Orioles had fifteen guys out there at 4:15. I walked by their manager, Earl Weaver, and said, "What did you do, sleep here?"

Weaver laughed. "You can tell you guys are going good," I said, "because you can't wait to get to the ball park."

"Yeah," Weaver said. "You guys had that feeling last year. When you're in first place, it's fun."

They had fun during the game, too. They beat us, 8-4. Magic number: Eleven.

September 6

Guess what? We beat the Orioles today—and nobody really cared.

The most important thing for us was the fine work a new man on the club did at shortstop. He's a teeny guy with a teeny swing, but he's got spark and speed. He stole a base, went from first to third on a single, and fielded very well. His name is Cesar Gutierrez, and, officially, we bought him from the Giants. Actually, we got him in exchange for Don McMahon, the pitcher we "sold" to the Giants after the trading deadline. If Gutierrez can keep it up, he'll help us a lot next season. Two of the things we've lacked all year are a slick shortstop and a man with exceptional speed.

September 7

We lost to Baltimore in the fourteenth inning today, and the magic number is nine. The Orioles' team batting average is above .270, which is incredible, but I realized today that a key reason for their success, beyond their batting and their great second-line pitching, is their defense. They've made only eighty-four errors, twenty-five fewer than we have. Last year we had the best team defense in the league. If you don't make errors, if you don't beat yourself, you have a lot better chance of beating the other team.

This is the first year since 1966 we haven't been fighting for a pennant in September. I miss it. Of course, we want to finish second because that will mean maybe a thousand dollars apiece, but finishing second isn't going to be any more soul-satisfying than coming in last.

It's all for money now—the money for finishing second and the money that individual achievement will mean in our 1970 contracts. The guys who've had a good year will be pushing for a raise. The guys who've had mediocre years will be pushing to avoid a salary cut. I probably have the biggest chance of anyone of getting cut, but in the back of my mind, I don't think I will. My batting average will probably be the same as last year's, and with a good burst I can come close to my home-run output. But my RBIs are down, way down. You work on those statistics in the last few weeks of a season like this. And you work on trying not to get hurt. My thoughts have drifted up north, and I'd hate to have my arm and leg in a cast for the hunting season.

September 8

New York came to town today and beat us, 3-2. Walking from my car to the stadium, I met Ralph Houk, the Yankee manager. Of all the managers in the league, Ralph is the one I'd most like to play for. He has the combination of qualities which I admire in a manager. He has intelligence, he commands respect, he inspires action.

"Cool weather got here just a few days too late," I said. It had been unusually hot during the Orioles series.

"Nobody's about to catch those people anyway," Houk said.

"You're right," I said. "They just got such a good jump early in the year that there was no way of catching them. But I thought if we could get a little bit close, we'd get some help from Weaver. He seems the kind of guy who might not be able to cope with internal pressure if things began to go wrong."

"That's the way I was thinking," Houk said. "But it never did get close."

I was impressed by Thurmon Munson, a young catcher the Yankees brought up from the minor leagues. I remember how pleased I was as a rookie when the experienced catchers went out of their way to talk to me, so when I came in from playing first base for my first time at bat, I said to Munson, "See what happens when you get to be older, young fellow. They send you out to pasture at first base. You can't do this catching work every day."

"Well," he said, "I don't know if I could play down there, Mr. Freehan."

Mr. Freehan. I thought it was only a couple of spring trainings ago I was calling Yogi Berra "*Mr.* Berra." I'm getting old.

September 9

We beat the Yankees today, and over in the National League, the amazing Mets beat the Cubs again. It looks as if the Cubs may blow their division title, and the guys were talking about that today. Specifically, they were talking about a certain Cub relief pitcher—our old friend, Hank Aguirre, the man with the black cloud.